THE SECRET PLAYER

THE SECRET PLAYER

THE HIDDEN WORLD OF PROFESSIONAL FOOTBALL

headline

First published in 2013 by
HEADLINE PUBLISHING GROUP

First published in paperback in 2014 by
HEADLINE PUBLISHING GROUP

1

Cataloguing in Publication Data is available from the British Library

Paperback ISBN 978 0 7553 6436 7

Typeset by Palimpsest Book Production Ltd, Falkirk, Stirlingshire

Printed and bound in Great Britain by
Clays Ltd, St Ives plc

Headline's policy is to use papers that are natural, renewable and recyclable
products and made from wood grown in sustainable forests. The logging and
manufacturing processes are expected to conform to the environmental regulations
of the country of origin.

HEADLINE PUBLISHING GROUP
An Hachette UK Company
338 Euston Road
London NW1 3BH

www.headline.co.uk
www.hachette.co.uk

Thanks to those who've helped out with this book.
You know who you are.

Contents

Introduction

I'm not a grass, a snitch, a rat. I didn't do this book for money. I've been fortunate to enjoy a great living out of football. I don't take it for granted like some players.

My name is nowhere near this book. It can't be, for reasons which will quickly become obvious. There would be at least four potential lawsuits in every chapter and I want to keep working in football.

When you see my name in the papers it will accompany the usual banal stuff about 'being fair to the lads' – just what I'm allowed to say and what is expected of me. A top footballer can never tell a fraction of what he knows and has seen, he wouldn't last five minutes.

My motivation was intense irritation at the nonsense written by outsiders who claim to know what really happens in professional football. The life I read about in newspapers or sanitised autobiographies is not the life I know. I've played across all four English divisions and represented my country internationally, spending eighty nights a year in hotels and travelling thousands of miles over land and sea.

I've played with and against the biggest names in football, seen what goes on behind closed doors as well as what goes on in front of millions but still gets missed. This is what, from my experience, is the true picture, though the names have been omitted to protect the innocent. And the guilty.

The season described here is a composite. Everything in these pages has actually happened in my career to date. Obviously, I couldn't tell the story of an actual season as you'd work out my identity pretty quickly.

The idea for the book came out of the column which I've been writing for *FourFourTwo* magazine since 2010, three months before the *Guardian* started their 'Secret Footballer'. I'm proud that last year it was nominated for Magazine Column of the Year – not that I could have picked up the award if I'd won.

I've been successful in concealing my identity, but there have been a few hair-raising moments. I once went to put petrol in my car when I saw the headline 'Premier League Orgy Shock' or similar on the front of a tabloid. I bought a copy to see what the lads had been up to – only to realise that the paper's story was lifted from my latest column in *FourFourTwo*. I don't know why I was worried, there were no names. And then a fellow player sussed me out. Or I thought he had – I'm still not sure.

Being a professional footballer has taken me on the most incredible journey, with major highs and a few lows. There are thrills, depressions, uncertainty and betrayal. At times it seems like the best job in the world, at others you hate it for being the ruthless dog-eat-dog world that it is.

Football isn't the glory, or even the beautiful, game for most of us professionals, even though we have glorious lives if measured by material possessions and rewards. Which, without wanting to sound like John Lennon in *Imagine*, is not how I measure my life. I've tried to tell it like it is.

Enjoy the book,
The Secret Player

July

I hate July, the worst time of the year for a footballer, the start of an eleven-month slog. It will be six weeks before we kick a ball in competition, six weeks of gym work and runs. And even when the season starts, we won't be anywhere near our fitness peak.

So I'm hardly bouncing my way into the first day of pre-season training at the Premier League club where, aged twenty-seven, I'm three years into a four-year contract. The kids are still in school so I drop them off before heading to the training ground on the outskirts of the city. Being a footballer in July feels like being out of sync with the rest of the world. You've already taken your main holiday, yet all your mates have yet to have theirs. Your kids are looking forward to 'the summer' when you've already had your summer and are focussing on 'the winter'. For family holidays, you have to take the kids out of school in June, something which does not go down well at all with the school, but what can you do?

I've had a good summer, but I've put on at least half a stone. It shows. I'm also nervous because I'm carrying a little niggling injury which was supposed to have cleared up over the break. It's not serious though, nothing worth telling anyone about, but skipping the last few rehab sessions wasn't the brightest thing I've ever done. Why did I miss them? Family holiday. I don't get much free time and the holiday had long been booked.

I've kept myself ticking over with runs and trips to the gym, but I'm not football fit, the type of fitness which comes from playing at least ninety minutes of competitive football a week. I went from intense training every day in April to runs three times a week in June. Then I went on holiday, where I drank and ate far more than I usually do. Isn't that what holidays are about?

I say hello to John the security man, park my car and walk into the dressing room. I bump straight into the new player who has been signed in my position over the summer for a substantial sum. I begrudgingly shake his hand and wish him luck, but deep down I'm looking for reasons to dislike him. He's wearing his jeans hanging off his arse so that's good enough for now. I'm also intrigued to know what he's earning – we all are. We've all heard different amounts and the consensus is that he's the best-paid player at the club. It's very useful for us to know what he's on, because we can use that figure as a bartering point when we come to negotiate our own new contracts. That's if we get offered a new contract, something I'm going to have to start negotiating before this season is out.

The mood is light hearted, though, and I genuinely hope the new signing settles in. I'm not being kind. If he does well then he can help the team do well and I'm confident that I can be accommodated. I know my place in the pecking order and I'm near the top.

The first day back is like the first day at school after the summer holidays, with everyone catching up. There's talk from the younger members about their lads' holiday to Marbella and what they got up to. Marbella is currently notorious among the ranks for being the venue for a memorable Premier League player's stag do. The stag got up to thank his sixteen friends.

'Except one,' he added, pointing to a member of the party. 'This prick has been sleeping with my fiancée, but I'm not going to let this little rat ruin our relationship.'

With that, he punched the guilty party in the face and that renowned ladies' man was completely humiliated. He just got up and left – with a black eye – hailed a taxi and caught the next flight back from Malaga to England. A boundary had been crossed – you don't sleep with a teammate's partner. Once admired as a right Jack the Lad, he was blanked by most of his teammates from then on and the word is that he's on the way out of that club. It would be impossible for him to stay in a dressing room when he's so hated. That's something you won't read about in the newspapers because nobody comes out of it well, not the fiancée for being unfaithful, the player for sleeping with a teammate's fiancée or the player for decking his teammate.

I've been on plenty of those all-male trips, but this year I went with my family to Portugal, where we have a villa. A lot of footballers have places nearby and I've seen José Mourinho on the local beach so he must be a fan of the area. Haven't spoken to him, just had the let-on that he knows who I am. You do speak to lots of other players, people you don't know but recognise and within thirty seconds of chatting mutual acquaintances will have been identified. The football world is a small one, you always know someone who knows someone.

My wife will take the kids back out there for a chunk of the school holidays, while I'll train, train, train and play, play, play. Other players have been to Dubai, Florida, Los Angeles and Vegas, the type of places where they can indulge in ostentation and girls with false breasts for a few weeks and not be judged every five minutes.

Vegas has become the destination for young top-level footballers because they can do almost as they please without anyone blinking an eye. If you act big time in Marbella then you'll attract attention to yourself among all the Essex hairdressers and plastic wannabe gangsters.

Dubai is too restrained. In Vegas nobody cares. Vegas ticks all the boxes. You can fly direct in business class and have your pick of some of the best hotels in the world. Drink and girls are on tap, a chance to gamble among the real high rollers and go to top nightclubs. The girls in Vegas are out for a good time and it's not difficult for a rich young man to pull. Impossible not to, really.

All a long way from where I am now, but a quick glance around the dressing room tells me I can relax. There are some noticeably big bellies on display and I've obviously been restrained compared with some of my colleagues who will divert most of the flak away from me, but nothing like what happened last year.

Players start thinking about their holidays in March, and everyone wanted to know the day we would be back in pre-season training so they could book their vacations. The players asked the captain, who didn't know. He then asked the first-team coach in training.

'Holidays?' said the coach. 'You lot should be focussing on the remaining eight games.'

'Don't give us that,' said one player. 'The boys want to know when they can get on the plane.'

The coach wouldn't divulge the dates and maybe he didn't know, but a few weeks later at an end of season awards function, he'd had a few and let it slip to the captain that we were back in training on July 6th. The captain duly passed it on and everyone was happy, especially one defender who would now be able to go on his mate's stag do in Vegas. He duly paid for the trip.

A week later, after the final training session of the season, the manager dropped the bombshell that we were to be back in on July 2nd.

The defender, particularly, was distraught, but he wasn't giving up easily. He went to see the manager and told him that his wife had booked a trip to renew their marriage vows. He explained that he understood that they were coming back on July 6th. The manager wasn't happy but gave him permission to go because it was a special occasion and also because his marriage had seemed rocky in the past. Looking him squarely in the eyes to show he wasn't a soft touch, he said: 'Don't let me down by coming back unfit.' The defender thanked the gaffer profusely and promised that he'd be back looking like a whippet.

Three days after everyone else had started pre-season training, he returned, red as a beetroot and wearing a stained Caesar's Palace nightclub T-shirt which had seen better days. He looked exactly like he'd only just returned from Vegas on a stag do and all the lads were laughing like drains.

We were then informed that we were going to do some intense running, the most difficult of the pre-season so far. The conclusion was a punishing two miler through local woods, to be completed within a challenging set time. We were on our hands and knees at the end. Ten minutes after everyone else was home, there was still no sign of the defender. The manager was furious. Finally, the player came through blowing through his backside. He could see that the manager was crimson with rage and tried to explain that he had blisters 'as big as pies'. The manager was having none of it, muttered something about fining him and told all of us that we would never be given permission to come back late for pre-season again.

Some people might say this is disgraceful, that highly paid athletes should have more self-discipline. Most footballers have drunk and eaten a lot less than the average man in the street of the same age. When most teenagers are discovering girls and alcohol, potential professional footballers are avoiding both, watching their diets, training, training and then going to more training. When you become a professional, for only a couple of nights a season, a few weeks a year, you get the chance to let rip. And many grab it with both hands.

I've not seen most of the lads since we played our final

game of the season in May. I'd class three of four of my team-mates as friends and I've seen them over the summer, but my close mates are the lads I grew up with.

There's been speculation that one or two of our best players are leaving so we have plenty to talk about.

'What you doing here?' our right winger is asked on more than one occasion. He's been linked with the biggest clubs and he smiles. 'Who have Liverpool got first game of the season?' chips in someone else, about the club the papers think our winger's joining.

Nobody gets on his case because he's a player who has a chance of going to a bigger club and earning more money. Most are probably thinking 'You lucky bastard' but until he goes, he's one of us. The usual scenario is that the player has probably requested a transfer and the manager has told him that he's got to get a replacement in before he's going anywhere. While the manager might think he's in control, he's not. A big bid for the player might be accepted above his head. I've seen a player sold against the manager's wishes only to line up against us at the start of the season and score a winning goal. Talk about rubbing salt into an open wound.

Until now, the first-team coach has been organising things in the dressing room. The manager only comes down from his office when we've all settled down by our new travel kits, which are nicely hung in our usual spot. Not everyone has a usual spot. The three young professionals in the second year of a two-year contract are now in with the first team and sit together, closest to the door. They have left the relative safety of the other dressing room at the training ground, the one for apprentices on £80 a week and first-year professional players on £600. Now they are with the big boys, aiming to push on in the second year as professionals. They'll be the lowest-paid pros at the club by a distance until they can establish themselves in the first team. These youngsters are ripe for abuse and they know it, but they've not got where they are by being push-overs and they'll give as good as they get. At the other end of the pay scale, the new signing sits next to them.

The manager walks in and the noise level drops. He looks well in jeans, loafers and an open shirt. It's not just because he's tanned, he's nothing like as stressed as he was at the end of last season when there were worries that we'd go down.

He welcomes everyone back and updates us on a few things. First he introduces the new players and the rest of the lads give them a little applause. The newbies nod a thanks in return.

The manager explains that the gym has been improved over the summer and will be ready for use in two or three days. There are a few more details about our pre-season games and forthcoming tour to Scandinavia.

The manager keeps it brief, but he finishes off by telling us that we're going to do better this season than last. He confirms what we already know – that there have been transfer requests. It's a given that there will be changes from the twenty-four players in the dressing room between now and the first day of the season in mid-August. Two or three will leave and two or three new signings will arrive. That's a lot of phone calls and negotiations in which the manager is usually involved. That's why the annual team photo is usually not taken until the final week of pre-season, another morning of high-jinks.

He tells us that the coach and fitness lads will be sorting things today and with that he's gone. He's always busy, even when there are no games. We change into our box-fresh training kit and the physio calls us individually to weigh us in an adjacent room. In turn, he's called every name under the sun because he's got bad news for almost every player. The fitness coach has been slaughtered ever since one of us saw his business card. He had more letters after his name than his name itself and he has about five degrees. Yet we joke that all he does is weigh us. My eight-year-old boy could do that, whereas the fitness coach has been doing classes to study how to weigh people for fifteen years.

This is his busiest time of the year and while he'll get hammered by the lads collectively, I often speak to him one-on-one to gauge his ideas. It's not good to show the lads that you are taking nutritional advice seriously, but, on the quiet, I have found it useful.

We all walk towards the training pitches and past the players' car park where the average price of the cars is just shy of £60,000. It's a given that your car will lose a grand a month in value.

That average price is only brought down by the nineteen-year-old midfielder's white BMW coupe which he's acquired over the summer. His insurance costs as much as the car itself, but that's the least of his worries today. Someone has written that his mum 'takes it up the arse off the milkman' in the dirt on the side of the car. Serves him right for not keeping his new second-hand car clean.

Range Rover Sports with blacked-out windows proliferate, but these cars don't get used in any transalpine races. No, they do the run to the private school and then the five-mile drive to the training ground on the edge of the city.

The groundsman, old Terry, has the pitches like bowling greens. You'd expect that in July, but they're like that in February too. He's in his fifties now but has been at the club since leaving school. He's not the brightest and thinks Holland and the Netherlands are two different countries, but he's a great groundsman. He usually gets pelted with footballs by the players who use him to find their range. Terry scuttles off towards his shed, muttering the names of past club legends and how they would have never behaved in such a disrespectful manner, but he knows he's liked.

Terry glances round to see the superstar forward urinating by the bushes on his prized pitch before training starts. We really like Terry and he's very popular, but we also like aiming footballs at his head and winding him up.

We'll be out for a couple of hours for that first session. It feels good to loosen up and we enjoy the rare sun. There's not much ball work in the first few days, more running. But gone are the days of long-distance runs through local parks and villages. I saw many a star player not take those runs seriously by jogging along at the back. What could the manager do? Drop him?

Everything is now measured by heart rate and a long-distance run which is designed to force your heart rate to reach a level and stay there. A combination of springs, strides and jogs will be more effective as your heart will get used to different levels – like in a game of football.

A few photographers and TV cameras will be allowed access to part of the training session so that there's evidence that we're actually back training. Seeing new staff faces about is unusual, because aside from the other players, a footballer may only be in contact with no more than twenty people a day at the training ground. That would be the working environment, the coaching staff, the physios, the kitman. Then there are the laundry girls, cleaners and canteen girls. You might see the chief scout knocking about, but it's a small group and nothing that goes on in it can be kept secret for long.

One regular visitor is the female yoga teacher who comes in once a week. A few of the older players are really into it – look what it's done for Ryan Giggs –and claim that it helps them stay more supple, but we're all convinced that they only go to look at the teacher's tits because that's all they talk about. One of the lads has slept with her – she's apparently mortified that alcohol blurred her professionalism and she got suckered into being another notch on a footballer's bedpost, the one thing she wanted to avoid when she started the job – but she's not alone. The same player has also slept with one of the massage girls and she gets ribbed as mercilessly as he does about it.

'Are you up first?' we'll ask him ahead of his massage session. 'And should we give you a bit longer than the rest?' He laughs it off, the masseur goes scarlet.

The manager wouldn't appreciate that his dependable right back's conquests include both the yoga teacher and one of the masseurs, not that he knows, nor is he a saint himself. Or so we've heard.

On one pre-season tour, he caught a player bringing a girl

back to his room when the players were not supposed to leave the hotel. The manager sent him to his room and then invited the girl to his own room for a night cap.

Your main aim in July is to get to that first game in August without any injuries and to be in the starting eleven for the first league match. Everything is geared towards that, yet those who don't make it can take comfort that the team which finishes the season is often very different from the one which started it.

You are reminded by how lucky you are not to be injured every day when you see your injured teammates in the dressing room. That's why I'm keeping my 'niggle' quiet. It's an inflamed Achilles injury, nothing which can't be sorted with anti-inflammatories during a game. It's a struggle until I get going in training and needs ice afterwards, but nobody needs to know that. Some managers look for any excuse to drop a player and I don't want to give my manager that, especially after he's signed a new player in my position.

The first week's training has a bit of ball work, but we won't start having eleven-a-side practice matches in training for at least a week. After two weeks we'll play pre-season friendly matches at a local non-league team, whose ground our club uses for reserve team fixtures. That will be part of the deal for them staging reserve team games and they fill the ground with 2,000–3,000 fans, almost all of them ours, paying £8 each. That goes a long way in non-league.

All twenty-four of our players will be involved – most players will play forty-five minutes each – and we'll look down on the non-league players like they're a piece of shit, the ones who didn't make it when we all have. You might know a few of them because they used to be trainees at your old club and they'd be a bit nervous because they would hope to avoid getting hammered. Games like that are not about results, no matter what the fans want. Pre-season results mean nothing. I've been at one club where we've won all eight pre-season matches and then been relegated. And I've been at another where we had a stinking pre-season and yet the club went on to have its best season in years.

Not all pre-seasons are meaningless, but not for the reasons you'd suspect. We played one game against a non-league side which had an extra edge that only a few of the players knew about. One of our players had been caught sleeping with the girlfriend of the non-league captain. Captain cuckold wasn't happy about it – as you wouldn't be – and the game had an edge from the start with two-footed challenges aplenty and everyone having to look out for each other. The referee, an experienced local Football League referee, couldn't understand the animosity and had to call the two captains together for a stern talking to and we managed to escape serious damage.

Players pick up little niggling injuries in pre-season as your body gets used to training every day. It's not a problem because you won't be risked in a match which means very little.

I don't like pre-season tours now because I don't like being away from home. I spend enough time in hotels as it is, but I used to lap it up when I was younger. All that travel to new and exciting places, staying in posh hotels and playing football at the same time. You tire of them as you get older, especially

17

as the top clubs have started playing further and further away. A twelve-hour flight to Asia takes days to recover from, no matter what official club press releases claim.

Scandinavia was always a favourite destination pre-season, close, clean and not too boring. The standard of football was high and perfect for us because the local sides were in the middle of their domestic season. Oh, and the girls are beautiful, too. What goes on tour usually stays on tour. I'd estimate that 30% of players are completely faithful to their partners. Then there's another 30% who are opportunists who would have a one night stand if they knew they could get away with it. Then there's the rest who are routinely unfaithful and take full advantage of one of the perks of being a famous footballer by sleeping with anything including a barber's shop floor.

On my first pre-season tour, the players went to a bar on the last night and ran up an enormous bar tab without thinking about how they would pay for it. That might sound strange given how much money the lads earn, but few of them actually carry cash about on those tours because everything is done for you. One player offered his expensive watch as a guarantee. The barman knew who we were and was fine with that. Except the player had brought a few watches away with him and forgot about giving one of them as a guarantee after several beers. The bar owner called the police, who came to see the manager. The players were all called down to be confronted by said manager waving a watch.

Another player, who was married with two kids, slept with a girl on the last night of the tour. She gave him two prominent love bites on his neck. He realised this the next morning and went into a mad panic as we were supposed to fly home. He started scratching himself on the coach to the airport and told his wife that he'd cut himself shaving. He got away with it.

We go to Scandinavia this year for three games in two countries, two of them against teams I've never heard of. One of our main sponsors is based there and I think they've funded the whole thing. We have to do a few corporate functions out there with them, where we're the guests.

In the games, we get passed off the park by all three teams. They're in the middle of their season, their fitness levels much higher than ours. It's good for us to do some chasing in a real match situation. Technically, they're good too, but none of the players will be good enough to get in our team. They don't have the same technical level, the extra 5%.

Pre-season tours could be a source of tension. Too much testosterone in one place for too long and they're as long as three weeks now. Personalities start to irritate you and you can't escape and do your own thing. I spoke to some of the Man United lads who'd been on a long tour to Asia. They couldn't leave their hotel floor and had security guards by the lifts to keep fans out. It came to that after a few of them – not even really famous ones – got mobbed when they went for a walk in a shopping centre. They had 20,000 fans watching them train and people pretending to be hotel staff by dressing up in cleaners' uniforms so that they could get to the floor where the players were.

I've never experienced that level of restriction, but I've seen the tension drive people mad pre-season. Think of it as an extended school trip. The petty bullying and jibes are only amplified by bored boys who don't know how else to entertain themselves or let off steam.

A few years ago, one player, a bright lad who wasn't your typical footballer because he read books and newspapers with no red on the masthead, was getting slated. He could really handle himself and would put other players down with his superior intellect, but one lad kept jabbing away. He'd say things like: 'It must be five minutes since you've rang your Mrs,' or, 'You've got a speck of dirt on your boots, goody-two-shoes.'

It was as if the lad was jealous. He ordered him a full English breakfast to be delivered to his room at five-thirty in the morning and there was clearly a personal issue between them.

After one comment too many about his wife, the brighter player just snapped one day and pinned him against the wall after we'd returned to the hotel from training. The mickey-taking stopped.

Players tend to split into cliques on pre-season. Bluntly put, the black lads and the white lads or the English and the foreigners if the make up is a bit different. The English lads will be the ones who want to hit the town and down pints while on tour. While they are out, they wouldn't want to socialise with the fans either, because most of the types who go on pre-season tours are anoraks, sad bastards with nothing else in their lives apart from standing on train platforms. I realise that sounds harsh, but it's true. They might say to us that they have come all this way to support us and the players might say how much they appreciate that support publicly, but their presence makes no difference at all. In fact they can be a pain in the arse and you'd try and restrict interaction to a let-on. Give them any encouragement and they'll come up to you and say: 'How many goals will you score this year?' Or: 'I hear we're signing such and such, is that true?' It's a one-way conversation all the time, with them keen to glean as much information as possible so that they can put it straight on the internet.

I have time for fans. I know how important they are. I appreciate their support and know that they pay my wages, but you shouldn't try and get too close because you'll get burnt. Burnt when what you think is a normal relationship turns out to be one where they ask you for tickets all the time and expect them for free, burnt by fans who are inherently fickle and will turn on you at precisely the time when you need their support.

We played in Spain one pre-season and then it wasn't just the anoraks who followed us. A lot of lads from the city came along for a jolly and they could be quite aggressive. So, rather than ask how many goals you thought you would score, they'd say: 'Are you going to fucking improve the number of goals you get this season?' This conversation might take place on a night out or at the airport. You can't be all cocksure and arrogant with these lads because you'd be likely to get a dig. Instead, it's better to instigate conversation and ask them how their trip is going and whether they've found any decent bars. Never give a fan your phone number or you'll have a life of misery and requests for tickets.

It very much depends on your standing with fans. In any team there will be a couple of current terrace heroes, time-served club legends and just as many scapegoats with the fans on their back.

And how you are perceived is down, in part, to how the media treat you. Those journalists who are assigned to cover your club enjoy decent access on pre-season tours. The manager might even have a beer with them, feed them a few stories to keep them on side. As a player, I would trust those journalists in-so-far as what goes on tour stays on tour. They wouldn't be looking to expose you because you were kissing a girl in a bar because they're only interested in writing about the football, but the minute you become *persona non grata* at a club, they'll be the first to slate you after being skilfully briefed by the club. Nobody teaches you this at coaching academies; you tend to learn the hard way. Not that I'm thinking too negatively as the worst of pre-season is well and truly over for another year and August approaches. I've started to feel good and confident about what lies ahead. The mood is good among the players. Now I'm sounding like one of those cliché-spouting footballers talking to Sky Sports.

August

August, the most optimistic month in football, when, for a few games at least, last season's slate is wiped clean – almost.

The immediate business for us is the rest of the friendlies. We've four left to negotiate against progressively more difficult opponents, finishing at home a week before the season starts with a premium friendly against a top team from the continent to pull in the fans and get us to the right level. The danger with these games is that such opposition can annihilate you because they could be at a more advanced stage of pre-season, or just far better.

One big-name player had his testimonial against a mid-ranking Spanish Primera Liga team. His side were getting destroyed, really being given a lesson. It wasn't the score line, more that their opponents had 80% possession. Tactically and technically they were superior. The testimonial player knew he'd have to do something to stop them trashing his big night and went in the opposition dressing room at half-time. 'Listen, lads,' he announced, even though it stuck in his throat to say it, 'you're taking the piss and are going to have to calm it down. We can't live with you.' I'm not sure how that was translated, but they went easy in the second half. The testimonial did all the home players a favour, they realised they had overestimated their fitness and concentrated on upping their levels in the last few weeks of pre-season training.

Friendlies can often be in the form of testimonial games. If there's a top-flight footballer with a few years in the game who hasn't played a testimonial against Celtic then I've yet to meet him. Celtic will bring thousands of fans to boost the gate, making it an occasion where everyone profits, unlike a lot of testimonials.

We played one Scottish team. It was a favour from our manager to a former club. Each of the players received a watch by way of thanks – the sort of watch the Shopping Channel would struggle to shift, horrendous plastic things. We had a drink after the game and I was one of the last to leave the bar. As I did, I saw at least eight watches had been left behind.

You get some weird gifts after testimonial matches, enough carriage clocks to keep any grandparents – and their mates – happy.

After one pre-season game in Scandinavia which I think was a testimonial for someone none of us had heard of, we were given a large wooden carving of a mobile phone. Telecommunications were big in the town. Initial reaction was: 'What the fuck is this?'

Later, for a laugh, one of the players went to the Scandinavian club's president after the game and said: 'Sorry for interrupting, but I've been trying to charge this up for an hour and can't work out how to do it.'

'But it's wooden, it's not a real mobile phone,' came the earnest reply.

There's always the suspicion that the manager is pocketing a few quid if we play friendlies at clubs he has been involved with in the past. If there are six or seven slots available for pre-season matches, the manager might have a say in two of those – a nice chance for a little earner, maybe.

Testimonials, though rare, can make players bitter. Firstly, if they don't get one when they think it's deserved, secondly, when they do happen and don't make as much money as they expect. Some players go into them naively because they have no idea of how much a football match costs to stage – why would they? In their innocent minds they tot up the crowd and multiply it by the average ticket cost. They think they are about to earn £300,000 and feel let down when it's half that. One player, a major name at a big club who played with me, really got the hump. He said that they charged him for ball boys, new corner flags . . . as well as the people you'd expect (but he didn't) including the police (he thought the government paid for them) and the p.a. announcer (whom he assumed was a mate working for free).

All but the top Premier League clubs play in the League Cup in August – and most couldn't care less about it. You can include our team today in that. There's a chance of Wembley, but that doesn't mean much when you're playing away at Crawley Town in front of 4,000. Or, even worse, Crawley at home when 70% of the ground is empty and only two stands are open. Today we've the classic 'no win' tie, big club against a small club. I find it hard to motivate myself, and as I'm trotting out onto the field my mind is wandering, thinking that there'll be a couple of upsets somewhere and hoping we're not one of them. And half my teammates are quietly seething because they've been chosen for our weakened side. They all believe they won't be playing against our top Premier League opponents this weekend. Everyone's frame of mind is compromised from the start.

We're up against a former teammate who was released in the summer. He was a fringe player and has dropped down two divisions, where he'll probably be the best player at his new club. But proving a point to his old outfit is where his head is tonight and, with his chest puffed out, he's thinking: 'This is my big night, this is made for me to prove people wrong.'

He's carrying a grudge, but the truth is he wasn't good enough to play in our first team and that's why the manager let him go. He was lazy, he didn't make the right runs, he went missing in matches. His level probably is League One and the manager made the right decision, not that it seems like that tonight.

The ex-player blanks our boss which creates a nasty atmosphere as he used to be one of us, and then he has the game of his life.

I can't point the finger, I've done it myself. Played against a former team, had a blinder and wanted to milk every second of it. I was first in the players' lounge and last out. My issues were against the club rather than any individual, but it was a massive confidence boost to do well against the team who sold me. That was the club where the owner was asking the manager why he'd spent all that money on me, opining that I was 'shit'. The owner never said anything to my face and nor did the manager, but the manager told my agent that he was getting abuse off the owner and my agent told me.

So, when I left that club, I made it difficult for them. Clubs have to pay you up until July 1st and if you leave earlier you negotiate a settlement, with the first £30,000 tax-free. I made sure that I was as awkward as I could be, so it cost them more, even if it also cost me.

Even in the worst summers, the British weather can always throw up some fiercely hot days. A bonus for those working on their tans in the stands, but in the dressing room the made-for-the-shade Brits and the Scandis are sweating uncomfortably already. Not so my rival/replacement, but we'll see how he likes it once the temperature begins to plummet. Unlike a lot of continental players, we Brits are not used to playing in the heat; even the moderate temperatures of an English summer day take so much more out of your body. But he'll soon be needing his second skin (or whatever Nike call them these days when they claim their latest product will change the world) and thermal gloves.

I played an away game early in my time at one club in a heat wave and was marked by a top international. It was like a furnace out there and after an hour I was inwardly screaming, 'Get me off!' I would have been happy to be subbed. The fans weren't happy as I visibly flagged, I could hear the moans and the groans, their chants for the substitute, whose place I'd taken in the team. I didn't want another twenty-five minutes of that, especially as we were two goals down. I could have thrown a little injury to get off the pitch by signalling to the bench that my thigh was sore. You can get away with that two or three times a season. I can usually tell when one of my fellow professionals has decided it's wiser to leave the fray prematurely. I didn't do it that day. I would now.

The lower league players, on the other hand, are loving it. While we have little to gain, they have nothing to lose. If we win 5–0, it will be expected, while they'll come out of a 1–0 defeat better than us. They'll be the gutsy lower league battlers and all that bollocks. And they will battle. Our legs will bear testimony to their efforts afterwards. They're drawn away and get to play on a superb pitch in a big stadium. What better way to enjoy the occasion than by stuffing a load of big-time charlies?

A good manager knows how to deal with this. We once won a game 1–0 against a League Two side in a half-empty stadium. It was dire, we didn't play well and the fans were moaning. The manager's reaction surprised me.

'They were crap, the fans were crap and we were crap,' he said. 'Yet in spite of that you still managed to win. Well done.' That bit of shrewd psychology lifted our mood.

Good managers do simple things to win respect. I saw one come into a difficult changing room with big egos. He created a mini argument, a heated discussion in his eyes, with the strongest personality on his first day. We all took notice. Then he told us that if any player started waving his arms about and complaining after he was subbed, they should enjoy the moment and wave goodbye while they were at it – because they wouldn't play another game under him. Players got the message.

The same manager showed that he wasn't all about

aggression. Walking a hundred yards across the training ground on his second day, the new boss came up behind me and said: 'Tell you what, son, my old captain at XX couldn't get the better of you. You were his worst nightmare, you drove him mad.' That lifted me, big time.

Confidence is vital in football. It can't all be manufactured, mostly it comes from good results, but a manager should know how to keep his players confident. Some players need love, need to be told how good they are and can't handle criticism; others don't need to be told anything.

I've seen managers destroy a player's confidence by bullying. It happens less now and players are more professional and go through the Professional Footballers' Association (PFA) when there are serious issues. We have one lad here at the moment who has been dropped and is drinking too much and is not in a good way mentally. In days gone by, a manager could, and probably would, have ridiculed him, but the lad clearly has depression issues that can't be sorted out with a kick up the backside and maybe the PFA can help him.

I once heard a boss slate a player and the country he came from in Eastern Europe.

'You are everything that is wrong with your country,' he said in a steaming fit of anger at half-time. 'You're a shit player from a shit country and you're a shit person.' We all felt for his target.

I've heard many a manager say: 'You lot earn too much money, you're not fit to lace the boots of the lads you're playing against and they earn a third of what you do.' And I saw one manager completely lose it after a bad performance. He went round each player and pointed to them.

'Shit,' he said to one, 'Not bad' to the next. Then he almost squared up to one as he hissed: 'Don't ever fucking knock on my door again and ask why you're not in the team.'

He moved onto the next one and pointed his finger.

'Get your agent to call me so I can get you a move.'

'Disgraceful.'

'You'll never play for me again.'

Then he walked out. I don't think he was too concerned about losing the dressing room. I did see one player react on another occasion, when the boss offered him out: 'You think you're hard. Me an' you outside then.' The boss was hard. And so was the player. The assistant dived in between them to try and calm things.

I'm one of those who needs reassurance, I admit it. Some of the blackest periods in my career have been when my confidence has deserted me. It got so bad at one club that I had a word with the manager, who continued to play me because I was one of his best-paid players. I asked him, if we won the toss at kick-off, if we could attack the vocal home fans in the first half, knowing that they were likely to get on my back in the second, by which time I'd be attacking the away fans who wouldn't be chanting anything about me. He reluctantly agreed.

I did that last year, but I wouldn't have had the balls to do it when I went through a really rough four months as an eighteen-year-old. I was having problems, as is not uncommon at that age, and the debate in the media was about whether I was good enough to be starting or not. What the media says doesn't bother you as much as stick off your own fans – one of the worst experiences for a footballer. If fans really want to know what they can do to help their team, not booing and abusing their own players is my top recommendation. You'd think they might have been able to work that one out for themselves. And one of the best is receiving dog's abuse from away fans, because that shows you're a decent player.

I know of one top-flight player who could only play away from home, such was the stick he'd get off his own fans. It wasn't obvious abuse, more that hollow groaning sound when he made a mistake which reverberates so loudly around the pitch. It destroyed him. But I've also seen players destroy their teammates in front of the fans.

It nearly happened to me. I was having a nightmare in one game and got substituted after the fans were getting on my back, booing and singing for the subs. The manager capitulated and brought me off.

I shook hands with the lad who replaced me – you have to. Snub him and you'd be the talk of the club. He got a big cheer when he came on, which made it even worse, then he scored a goal and went to celebrate in front of the fans, making a point of pointing to his name on the back of the shirt. I was sitting on the bench thinking, 'You absolute arsehole.' I blanked him after the match, then had to face the journalists saying: 'You must have been delighted for X, coming on and scoring.' I lied and agreed, when I really wanted to say, 'I was gutted because he's a prick.'

The goalscorer was asked for his views. He should have said that I'd battled hard for the team for an hour, which I did. Instead, he said that he'd shown the fans why he was worth a start. Knob.

I went out that night. A fan came up to me and said, 'I wasn't one of the ones who were booing you.' I didn't believe him, but nodded along.

'Anyway, quality goal by X today,' he continued. I had to agree, but then I gave in to some of the spite and pettiness I'd been supressing. I told him that said teammate was always slating fans and that he was unpopular in the dressing room. I didn't make it too obvious, just planted a seed of doubt in his head.

I'm not proud of that, but my head was up my backside and it was personal. Players are the same all over. They're egotistical and want to be the main man. Wayne Rooney would be feeling exactly the same when Robin van Persie arrived at Old Trafford and took over his mantle as top dog at Manchester United. He could never admit that publicly, but trust me, he was feeling it.

We survived our match against the lower league standard bearers for the true spirit of football, winning by two goals. Hardly our finest hour, but job done. Now we have to face a bigger test, the players' lounge, where all the wives and girl-friends are together waiting. This is dangerous territory in any August, because you've just been on tour and your women, even the most trusting, are suspicious. In the last week some stories have begun to leak out, spreading through Chinese whispers – and we know the source.

One of our number shagged a girl on the pre-season and the team was laughing about it within the safe, closed confines of the dressing room.

Another player told him: 'Wait until I see your Mrs in the

players' lounge on the opening day of the season.' This is a standard empty threat and you can handle the banter because it's just you and the team, bound by the dressing-room code.

Usually. But someone here has told his wife that one of us has been misbehaving and she's let it slip to another wife in a rival WAG clique. In our dressing room currently there aren't divisive cliques – but our missuses are making up for that in style.

'I heard there was a bit of trouble on the tour. My Steve wasn't involved and your Dan wasn't either, but she (pointing to a rival WAG) wouldn't be so full of herself if she knew what her husband was up to.'

How quickly word has spread.

The shagger cornered the blabber in the post-match showers, grabbing him by the scruff of the neck and said: 'You fucking blabbed, you wanker. If this gets me in trouble then I'll break your legs.' No one intervened. He knows the score.

The players' lounge culture is dying out. When I started, both teams went in after the match. You'd have a beer and there would be a good social atmosphere in what was to all intents and purposes a darkened drinking den.

Players used to smoke and get up to all sorts. One lad, a very skilful international, had a unique party trick. He dropped a half empty pint glass from his hand onto his foot. Then he poured a beer into it from waist height, if not perfectly, then enough to impress. Then he brought his foot up, picked the glass up with his hand and necked the drink. I saw him do that in front of the league champions in the players' lounge, when every one of them applauded him.

A very rowdy group of players once memorably took over the players' lounge when I was a first-year pro. They marched in and drank as much as they could in forty-five minutes. Chasers were ordered and they even bought a crate for the bus. An intimidating bunch, they behaved like a group of lads on a stag do. Players' wives were present with their kids, it wasn't the right place for fifteen men to let rip. I was mesmerised by them and their team spirit and so was our manager. A week later, he gave the captain £100 and told him to get the lads a beer in after a decent away draw.

Now, you're more likely to see players on protein shakes, but you still get people acting up in the players' lounge. I gave four of my mates tickets to one match and they enjoyed the hospitality pre- and post-match. By the time I met them, they were drunk and one had made untoward advances to a WAG. She told her husband who told me, very forcefully.

The WAGs need to be seen to be believed. If I ever turned to crime and planned a jewellery heist, I'd target a Premier League players' lounge. The WAGs are often dressed up to the nines in beautiful designer clothes and watches. It's a catwalk, where they weigh up each other and their Christian Louboutin heels with icy stares. They stick in their girly cliques and are wary of any newcomers who may pose a threat to them.

In the meantime, the most outrageous ones show off. One WAG told another in the players' lounge that she'd just spent £220 on a set of bra and knickers. The other wife, who was a down-to-earth woman, replied: 'I hope you wipe your arse before putting the knickers on.'

Not all fit in. I've seen many a foreign WAG alone, unable to speak English and desperate for her partner to arrive.

The other ingredient in this potent cocktail is family. The father of one player was particularly outspoken. He wasn't drunk, alcohol isn't served in half the players' lounges now. They look like nice city-centre cafes and serve food. But he was very opinionated and would dissect the game with his son after matches.

'So and so was shit, son, he shouldn't be starting,' he'd say, not realising that the wife of the player he was describing so charmingly was within earshot.

He would hammer the manager for his tactics, even if we'd won. How this dad was still working as a security guard on an industrial estate and not coaching a leading European football side, none of us knew.

Some of the lads found him funny, but his son considered him a liability and told him that he wouldn't invite him any more if he didn't keep his mouth shut and his very strong opinions to himself.

After a final warning, he cut a deflated figure, but the other players would try to get him to sound off: 'That wasn't good enough today was it, X?' Unable to resist, he'd blurt out: 'I'm under orders to say nothing, but I thought that X, X, X and X were fucking shocking. I'd get rid of them if I was in charge.' And away he'd go until his son arrived.

So you can see why some players can't be doing with the lounges at the biggest clubs and have bought their own executive boxes, which they go straight back to after the game.

My wife has never been interested in the WAG culture. She rarely watches me play and her focus is on the kids, though they can play in a crèche which the club provides for younger children. She finds the whole £900 handbags and two grand coats as false as their tits.

The away team seldom goes in the players' lounge now. There's a golden rule among travellers that the team bus leaves at a quarter to six. That's fifty minutes after the final whistle. In that time, the manager and a player or two need to do the media. The manager will also share a glass of wine in his opponent's office. Not that the plucky losers today would find us particularly welcoming companions.

Today our skipper is 'doing the media' with the manager; it's a relief that the rest of us don't have to work through the mixed zone.

The mixed zone, where journalists wait on the other side of a barrier, is somewhere I'll put my head down and walk through if I've played badly. If I've played well then I'm naturally happy to talk to journalists. Sometimes if I stop, the questions can be banal.

'How do you feel about winning today?' one will ask.

'Devastated,' I'll reply if I'm feeling sarcastic.

'What's it like being injured?'

'Wonderful.'

I once wore a Nike sportswear top with initials on it.

'New South Wales?' asked a journalist, 'have you been there?'

'Nike Sports Wear,' I replied, much to his embarrassment.

I've not had the greatest of games today, but then none of us has. I'm ready to go home. Sometimes the journalists won't take no for an answer.

After one match, as I walked back to my car a tabloid journalist badgered me 'for a quick word'. I wasn't in the mood. I'd not had a great game and couldn't be bothered having my words twisted. What was in it for me? Risk of putting my foot in it and not a lot more. So I said no.

'Just a few minutes,' continued the journalist. 'You said you'd speak to me last week.'

'I'll do it if you make me the "star" man,' I replied.

'I can't do that, I've already sent the match ratings off,' replied the journo.

'So we'll leave it, then.' I turned away and continued walking.

'Wait, wait, I'll sort it,' he blustered. 'I can't change the star man but I'll give you an 8, the same as the star man.'

So I spoke. And he gave me an 8, which I didn't deserve. Later, I wasn't particularly proud of what I did, but I did it.

I'll sign a few autographs on my way out. I've been well brought up, I think it's a bit rude not to. At away grounds, the fans will be waiting for home stars, but away from home you'll still get requests.

Tonight I'll be with the family, avoiding any of the now myriad ways in which my underwhelming performance can be publicly rated. After one away game in which we'd been hammered, our manager made us turn on our earphones and listen to 606 on the way home. Phone-ins are 80% negative. Few people call to say: 'I thought he had a good game today, bye.' The callers were destroying us.

Had they made valid points, I would have taken them on board. To be honest, I had no respect for their views. I'd respect a fan who pays his money to watch his team, but we had fans who'd not even been at the game or even seen it as it wasn't televised, and they were slating us. Their opinions were worthless. They were coming out with the clichés that people who know nothing about the game of football spout, like 'no heart or passion or desire'. Then there were calls for the manager's head and a wish list of players that should be bought but who would never have joined our club even if the Board could find the money.

The manager's quotes started appearing on Sky Sports showing on the coach's flat screen. We read: 'We were poor today and there will be changes next week' and sank further into our reclining luxury seats.

Players may check Twitter. They won't follow fans because they'll want to cut as much negativity out as possible. I've very rarely bought the local paper in my life – why should I waste time reading criticisms from people who are not as close to what's happening as they think they are when I'd rather stay positive?

It's not like they're accurate either. If I could change one minor thing in football, then it would be the scores out of ten in the newspapers. They're wildly inaccurate. How can one journalist accurately rate twenty-five people, as well as writing a match report? If a scout is sent to cover a game, he'll watch two or three players, tops.

The formations are often wrong too. Once, against Newcastle, I was asked to play out of position, withdrawn and out wide because I had a very specific role to get beyond the full-back. So one Sunday paper compared me, one-on-one, with Alan Shearer, listing how many shots we'd both had on target.

Ratings readers come up to you and say things like: 'You

had a good game at the weekend' when you didn't or: 'I heard you didn't play well,' when you did. For the player, they are just doughnuts, talking nonsense.

And where do they decide to pass judgement on your performances? When you pop to the shops and you try and do 'normal' things, because in your eyes you are normal. Yet in everyone else's estimation you're not: you're a rich, famous, young man and it seems like everyone wants a piece of you.

That may be a casual request for tickets from someone you've not spoken to for five years – though the person would expect the tickets for free because they think you're worth more than Bill Gates. Or invitations to parties or even kids' parties that your offspring wouldn't get a sniff of if you weren't a top-level footballer.

You have to be careful because you're damned if you do and damned if you don't. Go into your local pub and buy everyone a beer and you get called flash, don't and you are tight 'especially with all that money'. So when fans complain that they don't see footballers getting the bus to matches with them like in 1950, there's a reason we don't do it aside from the fact we have rapidly depreciating sports cars and don't need to use public transport.

When you try to be 'normal' you are also being judged all the time. A chance conversation which would have been repeated down the local pub is now amplified via the internet.

I know how this affected me and my response is the norm. I feel everyone is judging me. So I began to see my old mates less and less, partly because I live away from where I grew up, but also because I've seen a more exciting and glamorous world of great restaurants or bars and might want to enjoy them with someone who can afford it, such as a teammate. And because I don't want people coming up to me discussing inaccurate marks in a newspaper. How would you like it if someone publicly marked you for your job but was way off?

One journo used to really dislike a particular Arsenal player and would, without fail, score him low, as if it was a personal vendetta. They'd fallen out over something. The other players knew it and exploited every opportunity to drive him mad, pinning the ratings up in the dressing room, his pitiful score ringed in black marker. If he tried to fight back by saying he'd had a good game, the others would merely agree that everyone in the stadium knew that, but millions more would go by what was in the paper.

A footballer has to do what he can to avoid the constant tide of slagging off. Kevin Davies took himself off Twitter because he wanted to avoid negativity. I can see where he was at.

A lot of people use football as a place to vent their frustrations with the world. For some, it's a call to a radio phone-in to moan, for others, two or three hours away from their cage at home where the Mrs tells them to go and release their frustrations at the football. It's not like us players can answer back.

You see a lot of very odd people at football matches, social misfits who feel at home as part of a football crowd. You see them close up, shouting out their negative crap every week, from kids to pensioners. I swear football clubs should receive government money for providing a safe environment for these people every few weeks.

You feel like fans are out to have a pop at you because

they usually are, with the standard nonsense about paying your wages and how you should have more pride in the shirt – though the abuse is way less in August because the high hopes are still there.

Instead, our uncertainty comes from the August transfer window. We might be on that same bus back from the match and the manager is quoted on television saying that he plans to bring in a couple of new signings. That usually means a couple of departures and five or six of us wondering if we are in the hat. A club would tell our agents rather than us, though if we asked a manager directly he'd likely tell us.

I had a call from one agent to say that my club were prepared to sell me – and the next morning in training the manager acted as if nothing had happened.

Or you might be one of the players hoping for a move to a bigger club with a better paid contract. So, you tell your agent to see what he knows or what he's heard. Sometimes they'll know that one of your teammates is moving before you or the manager knows, because a deal has been sanctioned by the chairman. That can lead to a breakdown of trust between chairman and manager.

Other times, I've sat there thinking: 'My life could go anywhere here. I've just bought a new home and my kids are settled at school. My wife has finally settled and I might have to tell her that we're moving 200 miles away next week, the first six weeks of which I'll be there living in a hotel and she won't be.'

That's one reason why footballers don't move their families around with them all the time. Roy Keane moved his family and five kids from Cheshire to Suffolk after he'd been criticised for not bringing them to Sunderland in a previous job. So he uprooted them from their family home and they lived near Ipswich. Then he lost his job in Suffolk and had to move them all back.

Another reason is that contracts have changed, with one- and two-year deals being the norm when it used to be three and four years. If you have a four-year deal then you will be inclined to move your family – four years is a good chunk of time and it's worth the hassle of putting your kids through a change of school. The club usually helps with the move. If you get a one-year deal then it's not fair to uproot them.

So families stay put and most top-level players rent or buy a flat in the city where they work. That's more practical, but it leaves hours of time to kill and boredom kicks in. I've seen it happen many times.

At one club, four or five of the players would head off to the nearest brothel most days after training. They called it 'The £50' because the prostitutes would charge £50 regardless of the status or requirements of their clients. It became so routine that the players got to know the girls well and ended up going there for a cup of tea. After an hour with the girls, they would spend a couple of hours in the bookmakers to socialise rather than because they were addicted to gambling. I know one player – a star – who used to drive to a nearby seaside resort and spend the afternoon putting £1 coins in the slot machines. Winning barely mattered, killing time did.

Because professional footballers are free in the afternoon, they end up meeting other people who are free in the after-noon – and usually the wrong sort, people who work in or own nightclubs, people who like to hang around with footballers. Away from their partners or families, too many players start seeing other girls. Footballers know it's not right, but they have to abstain from drinking, smoking and drugs if they are going to succeed. Many feel they should be allowed at least one vice – women.

Thirty years ago players would kill time by heading to the pub, especially if they were given a day off midweek. That has changed. You can't go in the pub on an all-day session now, fill yourself with poison and expect everything to be 100% the next day.

There are more innocent pursuits. While a player visiting a museum or theatre would be considered an oddball, they might get away with going to see a film. More likely are extended sessions playing computer games.

A lot of the lads play *Call of Duty* at one flat or another, whiling away the hours on that or another game – it's usually football or war. There's always the internet but Facebook is a no, no as there's too much potential for trouble. Twitter is more private, but full of idiots talking nonsense and it can come back to bite your backside.

Other players go shopping, compulsively buying designer clothes or cars which they don't need. I once spent £600 on a Gucci jacket which I stopped wearing after a month. At the local BMW franchise salesmen, eager for their cash, will talk cars. If the franchise has a fit girl on reception then it makes it a more appealing place because they have the challenge of trying to chat her up – it's the competitive spirit you see. Some of the busiest car showrooms are in areas where there are a lot of footballers like Wilmslow in Cheshire or Chigwell in Essex. Selling to footballers is easy because they are rich and some of them are not the brightest of customers.

Boredom is always the enemy lurking around the corner, that's why players spend so much time together. I know a few Londoners who took apartments in the city where they were based. Their team were flying but their adopted city will never be compared with London, Paris or New York and they soon outgrew its limited attractions. They started doing practical jokes on each other for laughs. One player left a shit in another player's toilet. The macho thing means that players always end up taking it too far – and in this case the toilet owner got revenge by smashing the screen on the offender's expensive, giant plasma screen television. All for a laugh to relieve the tedium, you'll understand.

My current team are quite media savvy. The younger lads are all trained in the art of saying nothing. Our winger got burned last year when he quite rightly said that some of the fans need to support the team and not get on players' backs. That came out as him 'blasting the fans' and the fans retaliating on their high horses, claiming they'd do our jobs for nothing. The journalist merely blamed his office for the sensationalist headline.

Footballers get a hard time for sounding thick, but you can't take someone off a council estate and expect them to speak articulately like a middle-class salesman any more than getting that salesman to deliver an inch-perfect ball across sixty yards with no practice.

Footballers have to adapt quickly in an alien environment, where they are expected to speak in the language of a middle-class journalist and all before they are twenty. I'd like to see those journalists come on the estates of the footballers. Imagine one of them in Croxteth, where Wayne Rooney is from? They wouldn't last five minutes.

Professional footballers do all share one particular type of intelligence – the nous to make it as professionals when 90% of their peers don't. They need the intelligence to resist drink, drugs and girls and be committed to training, to listen to authority and interpret instructions. If not, they don't make it through a highly selective system, the top 2,000 of a game played by millions. Make it as a Premier League player like I did and you're in the top 100 English players, play for your country and you're in the top twenty.

That said, there are some really thick footballers. Sometimes being thick is an advantage for a footballer because he won't over-analyse everything and start a game mentally exhausted. And there's one player in every club who's really thick, funny and popular – like a current teammate of mine. The others don't pick on him, but he's so thick that he humours everyone and never works out why everyone's laughing.

We checked in at a hotel before one away match in a small English city. The receptionist gave the thick lad the key and said, 'Room 67'. He thought he was on the 67th floor and went in search of the 67th floor in a two-storey hotel. He claimed he was joking, but he wasn't.

Another time, he finally got to do a radio interview without a minder about winning his race to come back from a foot injury for a big match. The journalist asked him about the type of treatment he was getting. He didn't really know, but wanted to sound intelligent and replied:

'I've been with the osteopath.'

Quite why he said he'd been to see a back specialist for a bruised foot, I've no idea.

On the pre-season, he was in the casino and kept lumping chips on red. And black. At the same time. He claimed that he was covering his back, but all he was doing was risking losing everything if the ball stopped on green.

He's not alone. On a trip to a racecourse at another club of mine, a few players brought their mates along. A couple of dodgy characters were present, including one who was selling counterfeit £20 notes for a tenner. I didn't buy any, but a thick lad from that team who wanted to be in with the bad boys put his order in for £200 of counterfeit notes.

Then he handed over £200. He honestly couldn't understand why everyone was laughing at him.

Really thick players, as opposed to just normally thick ones, get found out in training. The coach might put on a complicated session with specific instructions, such as a game with three teams or a game where you can only take two touches. Everyone will understand, bar the thickest. Someone has to take them through it, if they can stop laughing for long enough.

It's one thing having a laugh, another when a thick player makes terrible investments. We're not all property tycoons like Robbie Fowler. I knew a player on £5,000 a week. An 'advisor' told him that if he added an indoor swimming pool and tennis court to his large house it would add value. He spent the money, it nearly cleaned him out, and then he found himself in £200,000 negative equity when he wanted to sell because the property market had dropped.

But whatever their level of intelligence, players often commit financial suicide, especially when it comes to cars. They buy a new car each year, a £70,000 Range Rover which they change after 12 months, losing £30,000. They take bad financial advice too and don't really know who to trust. One player saw his investment portfolio reduced from over a million to a third of that. He knew he wasn't getting it back and, fuming, took to smashing up his financial advisor's office.

As I gear up towards the first game of the season, I'll do it with the wife and kids away on holiday, maybe with her mum and dad. I'll speak to them each day and Skype is great for keeping in touch, but I also enjoy the freedom. Some players enjoy it a bit too much and make the most of their opportunities. For everyone who gets found out, there are twenty who don't.

At one of my Premiership clubs, a teammate had a mistress. He promised her a day out in London and the cosy couple boarded the first-class section of a train one morning. Then his world caved in. Among the other passengers in the same carriage were several of the WAGs with the same idea. They made a fuss of him, but he was petrified. He quickly sent a text to the girl who was sitting opposite him, which read: 'Don't ask why or say anything. Go to another carriage now. I will meet you at the station in London and explain everything.'

Then he found a quiet corner and called his wife, who thought he was at training. He said: 'I'd better come clean now before you find out. I've gone to London to buy you a Christmas present and guess who else is on the train – the rest of the WAGs.'

AUGUST

His wife thought it was really cute. His mistress knew he was married, though she didn't appreciate it being rubbed in. Such as when they went into a Bond Street jewellery store later that day – with the player keeping a straight face as he bought a present. For his 'mum'.

Unfaithful players become quite expert at deception. There are a few in my current club who think they have covered all the bases. I have a lift into training with one of them, who has two SIM cards for his phone, two phone numbers. He calls the extra SIM his 'bat phone'. The second one stays in his car or in his wash bag. Monday morning, I watch him put the extra card in and the text messages began to buzz away. He reads them out to me. They start with: 'It was lovely to meet you last night' and, fifteen texts later: 'You scumbag, for sleeping with me and not even getting back to me.'

The girls who throw themselves at footballers want attention, money and fame. You can go to certain bars where footballers have a halo above their head. They look fitter and healthier than the other people because they are.

The wives? Some are like Sherlock Holmes and want to know everything; others turn a blind eye and don't want to know. They've got a great life, they want to pretend that their marriage is all it's cracked up to be.

There are plenty of good husbands and decent fathers who are faithful to their wives and children among the professional ranks, but there are also many exceptions. But whatever is on offer, only the lowest, as I've said, would ever shag a team-mate's wife or partner. At one Premier League club I played at, there were strong rumours that one of the key players was sleeping with the captain's wife. The two lads were close mates

– both hard, old school footballers and club legends. Despite being married, the one who wasn't captain would get his leg over anything female. He established a reputation around the city as being a hard-drinking womaniser who was out on the town three times a week. He was once asked to sign the chest of a female admirer and wrote: 'To X, you know it's not just for pissing out of.' Vulgar and disrespectful I know, but that was him. His lifestyle didn't affect the way he played one jot. He would die for the shirt and the fans loved him. He was a good character in the dressing room too. We could play at Old Trafford or Anfield and he was always up for it and ready to lead the charge. You need players like that when you come up against better teams.

The only person who was more respected was the captain, so it became a bit uncomfortable when rumours of the drinker getting off with his wife persisted. The captain had to acknowledge them and laugh them off, but it was all a bit humiliating for him and the whole episode always left more questions than answers. I still don't know if it was true to this day.

I've heard of it happening once or twice elsewhere through the grapevine. I wasn't stunned when John Terry slept with Wayne Bridge's girlfriend. It's rare, but it happens, as it does occasionally in normal life. I think some partners suspect that their footballers are cheating and, if they do, are more inclined to cheat themselves.

Because players moved around so much, football's not about what happens at one club, there is the equivalent of small village gossip.

One lad went to a wedding and met the partner of a former

teammate. He was away, they went back to hers and he merely turned the photo of the couple over in the bedroom before getting down to it.

Football is a world of few genuine friends. You can be really good mates with a colleague; you can room with them, be a godfather to their kids and then not speak to them five years later. Temporary alliances are forged rather than true friendships, but you don't realise that at the time. It's harder to remain friends when you live on the opposite side of the country and you are busy with a family.

A few days before the first game of the season, and we are lining up for the official team photo, in front of the best stand at the club. It's a pain in the arse. We stay behind after training and change into shiny, brand new kits before waiting around for ages as the photographer tries to organise our group. It's probably easier for him to line up a primary school class.

One year, a leading player refused to pull his socks up for the photo. The photographer politely asked for him to pull them up, like every other player.

The player refused, so the manager asked him. The player again said, 'No, I play with my socks down, it's who I am. I don't give a fuck what you want. My socks stay down.'

There was a ridiculous stand-off which seemed to last an age. The photographer considered putting him on the back row where you couldn't see his socks, the player stubbornly refused to move. His status as the main man in that squad – and probably the hardest one – meant that nobody wanted to challenge him.

Finally, with all the other players starting to moan, he

agreed to pull his socks up halfway. He's probably not the man to negotiate peace for the Middle East.

The build-up to the first game of the season is like no other, because there's such a long lead up to it. It's one of my favourite times, at least before the match. You get to go through the motions of everything you love about being a footballer; the parts you take for granted and then miss when you are away from them in the summer. It's the little things, like seeing the fans in the new shirts, some of them with your name on the back, gathering near the ground as you drive in four hours before kick-off. It's a great time, sunroof down and seeing faces that you haven't seen for a couple of months, like Ian on the door of the players' parking or Mike who looks after the security. He'll make sure one of his lads meets you when you park your car and then walks with you towards the ground.

I always feel a buzz walking through the crowds and hearing the comments.

'Do 'em today, lad'.

'Hope you're up for it.'

I get there earlier so that I've got more time to sign autographs for the fans who are there four hours before kick-off, or – as is more common these days – pose for a photo with a camera phone. I've no problem with them if they ask, but I don't like it when someone sees you in public and starts taking pictures or filming you without asking. You can tell them a mile off, the weirdos who stand four yards away at an airport carousel or petrol station and pretend that they are texting a mate when they're covertly and discourteously capturing you on camera. Drives me mad and I've pulled a few of them up on it. They always maintain that they are not filming, but you can see the colour drain from their face when you say: 'So you've just walked fifty yards to come and send a text standing next to me have you?'

You see some great fans outside the ground. Of course the oddballs lie in wait – those who have made up fifty professional-looking photos of you and have a slick permanent marker. They'd have you signing all of them if they had their way, so that they can put them on eBay and make what they can. I sign one for them, no more, no matter what they say.

There's a lighter side – usually kids. Today's highlight is a kid with full kit on and my name on the back. His mum stops me because the kid is incapable of doing it. He's become star struck and stares.

'You're his hero, can you have a picture with him?' she asks. The kid just looks at me aghast, struggling to comprehend the reality of the man on the poster in his bedroom and me, there, in real life. I just smile.

'Say hello, don't be shy,' urges mum as the kid stands rigid with fear for a photo.

The kid whispers something and she laughs.

'He wants to know why you are not wearing a kit,' she says. Bless him, he thinks that I wear a full kit all the time, probably because I'm in full kit when he sees me in magazines, on television or at the stadium. I walk to the next fan, without the kid ever saying a single word directly to me.

I've never had any problems signing autographs, like Ryan Giggs did when he was asked for his autograph outside Anfield. He signed it, only for the fans to rip it up in front of him. One man did stop me and hand me a piece of paper and a pen.

'Can you make it out to John?' he said.

'No problem, John,' I replied.

'I'm not John,' he said. 'John is my son. He likes you. I think you're crap.'

Cheers.

One former teammate, who didn't quite make it to Oxbridge, or a single C in his GCSEs for that matter, was really confused when a fan asked him to make the autograph out to Panagiotis.

'Yer what?'

'Pan-ag-io-tis, it's a Greek name.'

'You'll have to spell that for me.'

'P-A-N.'

The player didn't get far before he was scribbling letters out as he kept spelling the name wrong. It must have been the worst looking autograph ever.

Some of the cockier types used to sign their name as 'Pele' or 'Bobby Moore'. You may have got away with it in the pre-social media days, but not now. You don't take the piss when you sign autographs.

Then it's past Bob on the door, who wears a club suit and acts as concierge by the main entrance which also doubles up as the players' entrance. Bob has been at the club for fifty years and directs directors and special guests to a table to check in and get their pass, but I'm just waved through into the inner sanctum, past the photos of past glories and former legends. I nod at the various staff whose names I don't always remember, friendly faces who've been at the club years and will still be there long after I've gone. They want you to do well because if the players do well, they do well. Nothing beats the atmosphere around a football club when the team is winning; a run of three points makes so many people happy.

Finally, I go down the corridor into the dressing room for that wonderful smell of football, a combination of Deep Heat, the oils, the aftershave. The dressing room is a sacred place, the inner sanctum. The kits are laid out beautifully, as are your three pairs of boots, flip-flops for the shower and trainers. Then there are shin pads, the massage tables, the fridges full of isotonic liquids for that half-time sugar rush. They can all wait, for first we all eat a meal in one of the restaurants, usually three hours before kick-off.

No steak and chips any more. Now it's healthier, chicken and beans or spaghetti carbonara. The fitness coach or nutritionist takes our order a few days before the season starts and our match day meal will stay the same for the season – unless we want to change it.

The senior players scoff at sensible diets in football.

'Don't do this, don't do that,' they'll say, smearing lashings of butter onto toast when they've been advised not to.

Eighteen players gather around the table and the banter kicks in. Someone loosens the top on the salt pot and then passes it to a young player, who won't know what's what and he covers his food in salt. If the manager or his staff occupying a nearby table see this then they won't be impressed.

Regulations stipulate a club suit for a home game, club tracksuit for away matches. As we're at home it's suits and ties, but the jackets are off as we eat, while *Football Focus* is on television in the corner.

After eating, we gravitate towards the players' lounge, where someone from the commercial department, a pretty girl in her twenties who can get the players' attention, makes sure that we sign footballs and shirts for the various sponsors who are at the game. It only takes a few minutes. It's August – we're only too pleased to do it.

By 1.15 p.m., we're all sitting in the dressing room, reading the match day programme. Some managers name their team the day before a match in training, others at ninety minutes before kick-off. The current manager tells us on the day of the game. I'm not sure which I prefer, not knowing that I'm playing or the nerves that come with knowing I'm playing.

Before he does that, the assistant manager will come and call a player's name and say that phrase again that makes everyone nervous: 'The gaffer wants a word.'

We call that getting the curly finger. Everyone knows what it means: you're dropped, maybe to the bench or maybe not even that. One or two might hum 'Another one bites the dust'. In his office, the manager will explain to the player why he's leaving him out. A good boss will be honest and say: 'I think you've been sluggish in training this week' or 'I thought you were poor last week.' Good, if that's the truth. If the player is less confident, the manager might couch it in gentler terms, explaining that he thinks a different combination of players will be more suitable for today's game. No manager likes doing this, but they all have to.

There are no surprises left when the team is announced at

1.40. Only three of our team start getting changed, the three main men who know they are certain to start: our captain, top goalscorer and the goalkeeper. I'm one of the maybes, who gets half-changed.

One former teammate knew he was on the way out and was sub most weeks. The manager didn't even tell him that he wouldn't be playing because he probably thought he understood that he wouldn't be, given that he'd been sub for the previous nine matches. But the player was feeling mischievous and he made it hard for the manager as only an experienced pro can.

He got fully changed, shin pads, the lot. He sat on the edge of his seat tapping his studs on the floor, eager for instructions. You could tell the manager didn't enjoy telling him that he was sub. Again.

'But, gaffer, I can win this game for you from the off!' he said. Even the gaffer had to smile at that one.

A five-minute talk on tactics follows; it merely reinforces what we've already done in training. Some of us actually listen to it. The best team talks are short and simple. The ones which go on and on tend to be lost on players. 1.45, seventy-five minutes to kick-off, the stereo comes on.

The players usually chip in for a stereo, something nice like a Bose speaker which you can drop your iPhone into, before the start of the season. The kitman will collect the money and it's his responsibility to take it around the country so that the lads can listen to their tunes.

The captain asks everyone to write down five of their favourite songs which they want to hear in the dressing room. They will form the basis for the dressing room playlist for the rest of the season, a list as eclectic as you can ... be anything from Tupac to Olly Murs. At one club, Mambo No. 5 came on. The whole dressing room stopped. Except one player, who carried on jigging about.

'What the fuck is this?' someone demanded in disgust. 'Who has put this on?' We all knew the answer. The dancing Mambo fan denied it, but he got ribbed mercilessly.

My selection consists of house music, the more uplifting stuff. There haven't been any complaints, or at least not while I'm there.

An hour before kick-off, the assistant manager and the captain are off to the ref's room with the team sheet. The ref has a word and tells them that he'll look to them for contact during the match.

Then our manager's assistant does a refresher back in the dressing room, pinning notes of paper to the wall about who is marking whom.

We have fifteen minutes to ourselves. It's an important time for me. Some of the players will have a rub on their legs, others will take a shallow, hot bath to warm up their muscles. You should run the water to a depth of two inches and not do what Paul Gascoigne once did and run a full bath, complete with bubble bath. He sat there relaxing and telling everyone how great it was. Then he ran out onto the pitch knackered.

I like to spend this time stretching my back off. I'll lie on the treatment table and roll from side to side for ten minutes.

In the newer, bigger, stadiums, there will usually be warm-up space beneath the stand, space to jog, stretch and kick a ball. Some players go for that.

At 2.20 p.m., the captain shouts to the players and leads us out for a warm up together. We're in our shorts and socks with a training top rather than the team shirt.

As we leave the dressing room, the manager says, as many of them do, in my experience: 'Our game starts here. I want it right in the warm up and right from the first whistle.'

We run out of the tunnel and applaud the few fans who are in the stadium forty minutes before kick-off. Our warm up consists of jogging and dynamic stretching, that is stretching on the move. Gone are days of static stretches, you're trying to replicate what you'd do in a game.

Some ball work follows, playing 'keep ball' in 20 x 20 yard areas, where you play six-a-side and have to retain possession. It sharpens you up. The warm up lasts for about twenty-five minutes and we leave the pitch at 2.45 and sign a few autographs for fans near the tunnel. Managers frown upon that because they want you to be 'in the zone' and not have your head filled with distracting thoughts. A fan could say anything to you.

At one Premier League club, a large, hard-looking fan kept shouting the name of an England international who was on the bench. The player ignored him at first, but the fan wouldn't shut up. Finally, the player stuck his head outside the dug-out to hear what the fan had to say.

'You shagged my daughter on Thursday!' came over loud and clear.

The player was speechless, because he had actually had had a one-night stand – on Thursday. Everyone within earshot including the manager and the other players looked between the fan and the player.

'Go on, my son!' bellowed proud dad. 'I hope she gave you a good time,' to howls of laughter.

With only fifteen minutes to kick-off, the team are back in the dressing room. The shin pads go on, and any final superstitions are rehearsed. For some, it's as simple as putting their left or right boot on first; for others it's cold water over their face before every game or leaving the dressing room last. Or second to last. Or fourth. It all got a bit confusing at one club and the manager had a word about it. 'Superstitions are for weak people,' he said. 'Preparation is more important than superstition.'

I played with one goalkeeper who used to volley the ball against a light switch until he turned the light switch off. It could take him half an hour, so he'd start early. It was bizarre to watch.

Another player had to sit in the corner of a dressing room, home or away. He had to be in the corner. Another had to have precisely three drinks which he'd prepared himself before each game, part Lucozade, part water.

I'm not a man of superstition, though I did wear my collar up for a few months. My mates hammered me.

'You're trying to be Cantona,' they said. I quite liked it, but then the home kit was changed and the new one didn't have a collar.

Five minutes before kick-off, the bell indicates that we need to leave. Before we do, everyone shakes hands including the substitutes. You want them to feel as much a part of it as anyone and say, 'Have a good game when you get on.' There's no ambiguity, *when* they get on and not *if*. At that point, the manager, the man who makes that decision, bellows: 'Fucking come on' to get everyone hyper.

AUGUST

We leave the dressing room single file and wait in the tunnel, where the man with the microphone is trying to whip the crowd up. Television demands that you are kept in the tunnel for longer so that they can build up the drama. I don't like that, but if we take the television money then can we complain?

If you see anyone you know on the opposition team then it's rude not to say hello if they are standing in front of you. What's not normal is to ask, like one former Wimbledon player: 'What are you looking at, you fat cunt?' That was a tactic they used, along with setting fire to each others' clothes. They once put tape over the word 'Anfield' on the 'This is Anfield' sign and replaced it with 'bollocks'. Of course it was disrespectful, but they were going there to win a game of football, not be intimidated by Anfield's reputation. Nothing fazed them and they were a better team for it. And they won.

Whenever the announcer says: 'Please welcome today's teams' and I run out, it's the best atmosphere of the day. When it happens on the opening day like today, it's possibly the greatest moment of my season. The pitch is perfect, the home fans are full of optimism, the 3,000 away fans likewise. I wave to my family in the stand; it's easy to spot people when you know where they will be.

At that moment I love everything about being a professional footballer. I'm charged up and ready to go . . . and then the pace is slowed to a funeral march as we shake hands. Every player hates the ridiculous handshakes and the rigmarole which goes with it before the games.

It used to take a minute or two, now the whole procession from leaving the dressing room lasts three times as long. The handshakes might look tense and exciting at Old Trafford, but they're a pain in the arse at Burnley on a winter's night.

The lads who don't like the handshakes or don't like individuals on the other team walk the line offering their hand and making no eye contact. Some offer a limp handshake – they just want it over with – but I've never seen a hand not offered like Wayne Bridge or Anton Ferdinand did with John Terry.

One player did it very differently in a League One game. He'd dropped down a few divisions from the Premier League and he kept moaning about the standard. At an away game at a small club, he walked along the line with a message for each opposing player. They varied from: 'You're shit,' to 'Average,' to 'You're not bad,' or 'You'll be working in McDonalds's next year.' The opposing players were stunned rather than offended, while his own teammates thought it was funny.

The handshake should be scrapped. Anyone can do it before the game, but it's insincere. You don't really want to wish them all the best, but all the worst. What matters is that you can do it after the game once you've played each other, that's when they are worth something.

Our boys break away. Our opponents today favour the huddle. I can't stand them either. We tried at one club but when we got in it nobody knew what to say and we felt like knobheads. We also lost the game. There were no more huddles.

The captain shakes hands with his opposite – and, finally, the ref blows. The season is underway and at this moment the world seems like a wonderful place.

September

After the euphoria of the opening league games follows the anti-climax of the two-week international break at the beginning of September. International football needs to be played sometimes, but supporters find it irritating, if not bizarre, to bring a halt to proceedings so soon after the summer break.

All professionals want to do is play football. That's all we have ever done since childhood. That said, stopping may seem unnatural to outsiders, yet I for one appreciate the lay off, because from July 1st until the first weekend in September, it has been relentless. You never get more than a day off, so it's a bonus to have three or four days in the eleven-month slog of a season if you're not on international duty.

At the biggest clubs, international weeks mean an almost empty training ground, populated only by the unselected and the injured as most of the other players go and represent their country. The doctors and medical teams try to catch up on their paperwork, while training is less intense, with people like me doing some gentle work or maybe joining in training with the reserves. Briefly escaping the first-team bubble and speaking to players I don't see so much of is enjoyable. I feel valued when they ask my advice in the hope of improving – and one day pushing me out of the team. I've always tried to help players and had to laugh when one to whom I'd given a lot of advice came on for me in a big league game a few years later. He laughed too.

It also offers a chance to catch up with fan mail. There's a wall at the training ground and each player has a pigeon hole with his name on for his mail. Some are overflowing because the player can't be bothered with his mail, or because the player gets so much. The model professional will answer all.

I've always had quite a lot, up to ten a day at one point, usually straightforward requests for autographs. So as long as they send an SAE, I'll respond and then give the envelopes to Liz on the training-ground reception to post for me. If they don't send an SAE then they can do one. Do they think I'm a postman too?

Quite a few are begging letters, where the writer details their horrific life. They tend to go in the bin, especially if every other player receives the same letter.

I've never had any knickers sent to me like our number five. He opened an envelope from what he presumed to be an admiring female fan. He'd barely got the black thong out when the winger was wearing it on his head. Within a minute, the word was that a transvestite fancied him rather than a woman.

Many letters are, inevitably, from moaners. They always

start by saying that they've been supporting the club since the year dot, before explaining 'and I've never seen anything as bad as last Saturday'. They then go on to detail how the team can improve and suggest that I have a word with the manager about making sure the right back overlaps more and that he drops the left winger. These people are not joking; they really think that I can get the manager to change his mind. I can't.

One fan sent me a packet of Brazil nuts. I still can't work that one out.

If everything is going to plan at the club in early September, some enlightened managers let their players have time off, maybe a few days in the sun, a chance for a late summer holiday to Dubai or the Caribbean with the family, though naturally the schools aren't thrilled – again.

But other managers detest that idea and won't give the players more than two days off. That can infuriate the foreign players. One of the best managers in Britain would let players have Monday off, but want you in on Tuesday morning. Wednesday would be free again. To prove a point, one player hopped on a flight to his country, spent half a day there and then flew back to England.

To try and get more time off, the players would badger the assistant manager. 'Tell him that we need four days off,' we'd say. 'Tell him that the boys are looking tired and could do with a few days' break.'

I appreciate the break from work. I never used the word 'work' as a young player. I do now. It's a tough job in a hard, high-pressure industry. You need to try to be 100% every single day, that's not easy. Do you concentrate every minute of your working day? In football, if you slacken off, you will be noticed and it will go against you.

I've stayed behind at training grounds and I've been away on international duty. It's a massive buzz when you get called up for your country for the first time, for you and your friends and family. I got a call on my mobile from the England manager. I was half expecting it because I'd been playing well and the media were talking up my chances, but it was still a nice call to get when it came early one September.

I was nervous when I joined up with the England squad at The Grove hotel near Watford. I've stayed in some amazing hotels, but The Grove is one of the best, like a country estate and yet just outside London. It's better than other five-star hotels, with magnificent food, spa and golf. When I went for a meal there on my first day, I didn't understand half the things on the menu and looked for key words like 'chicken' before ordering.

My appreciation of the place was quickly soured when I saw the cliques: the black lads, the Manchester boys and the London boys. I felt like an outsider and not only because I was earning a fraction of the others. That became apparent when the players starting gambling. Some stakes were a modest £10 or £20 but some ran up debts of £30,000. There was a lot of bravado and boasting, with players anxious to show that they could afford to lose astronomical amounts. I made my excuses, told them that I didn't understand cards and kept my head down.

I've seen lads lose absolute fortunes at cards. A close mate, who has played many times for England, told me that he's routinely seen players write out cheques for £15,000 to pay for gambling debts. He also said he once saw a player run up even bigger debts on one trip.

The player who was owed the money said 'Don't give me the money, buy me a watch instead.' The watch he suggested cost the equivalent of the debt: £45,000. Maybe it was a form of boasting by players who earned so much money that they could afford to lose astronomical amounts, but it's a serious problem for some.

Players have been warned recently that they are not allowed to gamble on any matches in any competition in which they are involved. Family and friends of club employees are also barred. So a friend of a man who sells pies at the Emirates once every two weeks isn't allowed to bet. It's impossible to enforce and besides, the many players who like to gamble will always find a way. They aren't match fixing, either, they just like to bet on the one subject they know something about.

At one club, we had an informal bookie who was close to the players and would come to the training ground. I think he laid our bets with a local bookmaker. No names, only winners – and even more losers.

At another, a youth-team player was given £3,000 by the club captain to puts bets on. He missed the bus to the bookies and spent the whole weekend shitting himself as he would have been £15,000 down if the bets came off. The bets were not successful and he found himself £3,000 up – or 100 times his weekly wage at the time. That young player, who was very good, would become a notorious gambler. The gambling undoubtedly affected his career because he demanded – and got – several moves to different clubs so that he could get signing on fees to pay his gambling debts. That his family had to move with him was all secondary.

I've never been a gambler. Apart from the cost, I've seen the misery and destruction it can cause. But in every team I've played for there has always been the gambling crew. They sit at the back of the coach and play cards continually. Managers would turn a blind eye – most were not averse to gambling themselves.

We had a team day out at the races one year, a social occasion when most of the players were betting small amounts, enjoying the atmosphere. One, however, wasn't content with a flutter on the horses. He was on slot machines and betting on anything he could, even things he knew nothing about like American greyhounds. I actually pitied him. His personality changed from being a good lad to be around to that of an addict.

A few hangers-on came that day too, carrying false notes and I wasn't happy, thinking, 'Why am I associating with scum like this?' The same notes were used in a bar later that night until they were spotted and the bar manager threatened to call in the law.

The public tend to be shocked by revelations about the sums gambled by footballers, but it's all relative. With £40,000 a week earnings you are hardly going to bet £20, are you? Some of the top players do feel invincible and gamble stupid amounts. The levels among the England lads were legendary. Players were losing six figures on international trips, yet other players talked about it like a normal person would speak well of a mate who can 'handle' ten pints, a back-handed compliment.

Some get into a right mess. One really high-profile figure re-mortgaged his house several times to pay his gambling debts. Another has significant debts which have been passed onto criminal families who contacted the club suggesting that it might be a very good idea indeed for the club to pay the debt. There was always an 'or else' undertone. The strange thing was that his performance on the pitch remained largely unaffected, as if playing football was his escape from the gambling madness.

Players with long-term injuries can easily fall prey to gambling. They miss the buzz from playing and get it instead from risking their cash. At least they feel part of something.

I'm talking about isolated examples. Most players, even Championship lads on £4–8,000 a week, know that they can set themselves up for life if they are sensible with their money. They know they can pay off their very nice property and make some good investments. Gambling that money away isn't one of them, but I can understand why some players do it.

Gambling can be done anonymously. No one needs to see you scurrying off to a bookies, like in days of old. With so much dead time to kill in strange towns and as gambling is not as detrimental to your health as alcohol, it's no surprise that players turn to gambling to get a buzz. You can fail a drugs test, but you can keep a raging gambling habit quiet for your whole career.

I found that the novelty of playing for my country quickly wore off. It's nothing to do with money. You get an appearance fee, but that's peanuts. It's more that when you play for

England, the deal seems to be this – you leave your family for a week or more, you fly to a shithole country, you play with lads who are not as united as they could be because they barely know each other, you get slagged off mercilessly by the press, you come home.

Different England managers have tried varying off the pitch tactics. One got the players together at The Grove and said: 'If you want a couple of beers then you can have one or two tonight, but none of us tell the press. If you want to play golf, then tomorrow afternoon is the time for it after training, but don't tell the press. If we're all singing from the same hymn sheet then there will be no problems.'

The players had a drink that night in the hotel bar. I think it was the manager's idea of team bonding. Everyone ended up shit-faced.

Security is tight around the England hotel, but it is still open to other guests. Guests who would get in a lift with two footballers, one of whom was Paul Gascoigne. The other of whom would have his shorts pulled down by Gascoigne in the lift. I didn't play with Gascoigne, but stories about him were legendary among players.

The security lads could also be bought off if someone wanted to bring a girl in, but that didn't happen often. And the manager told them to turn a blind eye when a friend of the players sold dodgy DVDs – not porn, just pirated, recently released films which the manager thought would help the players pass the time. It's all iPads and downloads these days. I think the dodgy DVD man has been put out of business, another victim of the internet like record shops.

The media come to the England hotel for a press conference once or twice on each meet up, but autograph hunters aren't allowed beyond the main gates. The security largely do a good job of stopping the hotel being a free for all.

Until the new St George's Park training centre opened near Burton-upon-Trent in 2012, England trained at Arsenal's London Colney training ground, a top-class facility just fifteen minutes around the M25 from The Grove. All flights to away games would leave from Luton, a charter airplane in which the team would sit at the front and the press at the back. It's a way of sharing the costs, or, according to the journalists who reckon that their papers pay so much that they pay for us. At some of the biggest clubs, the journalists have been replaced by sponsors on European away trips.

Clubs have a big issue if you come back from international duty injured. Can you blame them? However I once went on international duty injured rather than miss out.

I had a problem with my knee and knew that I'd need an op. But I really wanted to go on the away trip – I'd not been an international for long and was still full of enthusiasm for it. I reported for duty on Sunday and trained on the Monday and my knee was quite sore. We flew to the lovely European capital on the Tuesday morning where we trained again. I told the physio after that my knee was not right and needed ice. I was out of the match and free to have a look around a historic city in the sun.

I went back to my club and told them about my knee. They put me in for an operation and I was out for four weeks. They knew I'd need an op, but I could have been a week or two further down the line had I not fancied being part of the international set up for a big game. I don't think the manager was impressed, but he didn't say much.

When you play for England, you get loads and loads of free Umbro sportswear every day in the hotel. The younger lads love it and keep as much as they can and hand it out to their mates.

One player saw an opportunity. He knocked on the doors of every teammate – all twenty-two of them – saying that the gaffer thought the sportswear thing was getting a bit excessive with players taking too much gear and that they had to return several items each. They were to leave it outside their hotel rooms in the corridor in half an hour.

The player then ordered a taxi to the hotel. He scooped up piles of the sportswear that his unsuspecting teammates had dutifully left outside, not wanting to appear as if they needed the freebies, you understand, and smuggled it out into the taxi, which he sent to a mate's house in London. There must have been enough for a sports shop. He got away with it too.

Another foreign lad was hugely talented, but a bit, well, thick. The big sportswear companies wanted to sponsor him as he was going to be a star and he signed with one of them. He was allowed unlimited boots and got a two grand credit for their main store. Most pro footballers go through between ten to twenty-five pairs of boots each season with all the training. The boot manufacturers don't advertise that do they? This lad ordered more and more and started selling £200 boots to teammates for £70. After six months his agent got a call. The sportswear giants wanted to know if there was a problem with the boots. The agent said there wasn't.

'It's just that he's taken 547 pairs of boots in six months . . .'

September is when you approach full fitness. That's when you can still chase a forty-yard ball in the eightieth minute like you can in the tenth. It's when you don't leave the field at half-time blowing through your arse and thinking: 'Thank god for that.' It's a wonderful feeling to be fully fit and you feel confident, which helps you play better. These positives feed off each other, but I'd estimate that I'm completely right mentally and fully fit physically only 30% of the time. The rest of the time I'm trying to get to that level – which is not always possible. You don't choose to carry any injuries, nor to have issues weighing your mind down. Nervous energy can deplete half your energy stores – you put pressure on yourself because you want to do well, want to impress. I've gone into some games shattered because I've been worrying too much. Every player is different.

The pitches are still perfect in September as the grass grows until November and the heat in the new stadiums – the bowls which allow little air circulation and can be stifling in August as I mentioned previously – is no longer an issue. In fact, some of the foreign players from warmer climes miss the heat, so clubs now have machines which are like sunbeds and replicate sun without giving you skin cancer and a tan fit for an appearance on Jeremy Kyle.

A bad start to the season will see the 'we just need a little time to gel' cliché trotted out by struggling teams and struggling managers. My current manager is a bit of a worrier. I've noticed it in the last few weeks as he's become more irritable with poor results. We've drawn one and lost one when, at the start of the season, we would have identified the two games as ones we should win. It's not a disaster as we're mid-table and that's what's expected of us.

He told one of the players off for wearing gloves in training last week and accused him of being soft. While never having managed myself, I've worked under several big names and can conclude that the greatest part of being a good manager is man-management skills. It's about saying the right thing at the right time, making players think and change their opinion, handling difficulties, getting the best out of individuals, from recruiting the right ones and deploying them correctly. How you deal with popular players bought in by former managers, players you might feel are past it. So many managers bring players in from their previous clubs because they can trust them. I've followed a manager twice in my career. I was the devil he knew and it helped him; he understood me and I was happy to join up again with him. Doesn't the same thing happen in other businesses?

Managers take a gamble buying any player because they don't really know his personality or how they'll get on until they start working together. They can eliminate that uncertainty by buying someone they know and trust.

On one such occasion, I was sitting at home, not enjoying life at a Premier League club. So I called a former boss and asked him to consider me. 'That's interesting,' he said. A week later I was signing for his team.

The one downside is that you are considered to be the manager's pet, which is only a problem if the manager is unpopular. Then other players don't trust you and think that you'll grass to the boss. At one such club where the manager undeservedly had his enemies, I told the assistant manager what was going on in the dressing room, knowing full well it would get straight back to the gaffer. I did that for the good of the club, because there were one or two devious characters who were trying to undermine a good, honest and hard-working coach.

I realised that they knew what had happened two days later when some of the other players refused to sit next to me in the canteen. I'm glad I did it, though, and I did it again. The manager eventually got rid of the bad elements and matters began to improve.

Players are some of the worst at appreciating just how many aspects there are to management. Anyone with money can buy players, not everyone can get the best out of them, appreciate when to administer a firm kick up the arse or bestow a day off. I would rate this above being tactically astute. The best manager should get you in the best mental state before you walk out on the pitch. He will watch everything that is happening at his club, soak all the information in and then make decisions on what he sees and what he's told by his staff. Sir Alex Ferguson watched everything at Manchester United's training ground. His office overlooked the car park and the training pitches. He could see who was arriving and when, what cars they were driving, what they were wearing. The best managers are the ones who are respected, the ones who cause you to put your back up straighter when you pass them in the corridor, as if the head-master is about.

A top manager should not socialise with his players, nor be all matey with them. And he should be the biggest personality at the club, not scared of a single player. I also believe that he should be the best paid.

Yet I've only had one manager who wasn't scared of some of the biggest personalities in his dressing room. He wasn't afraid to drop any player, not even his captain. You got in his team on merit, end of.

I don't envy managers and I would never want to be one. Once you get above a mid-table championship club, players have more power than ever. They're earning very, very good money, millionaires paid enough to retire on after a few years. They can afford to walk away; they don't need their wage to pay their mortgage.

A good manager will praise you after a bad game. Every player knows if he's had a good or a bad game, it's black or white, there's no middle ground. A manager can't kid you that you were better than George Best, but might say, 'What about that run you made in the second half?' accentuating the positive to encourage you.

There are other nonsensical clichés spouted about management, such as 'the manager has lost the dressing room'. Managers can't lose a dressing room because, quite simply, they never have control of it in the first place. Good managers have an aura which wins them only respect, but not absolute control. And no manager can command respect after a run of bad results.

Players will always try and take the piss. They'll be late for training, late for anything. Poor managers don't want the physio coming up to them and saying: 'So and so was half an hour late this morning'. They don't want the confrontation of dealing with a player in his office. Poor managers are paranoid that certain players have the ear of a (usually) interfering chairman – which they invariably do. Poor managers will play fans' favourites even when out of form because they don't have the balls to drop them. Better managers will have more control and confidence in their decisions – and are far smarter than their players.

You know when a manager has little control over his team by the reaction when someone is substituted. If a player comes off shaking his head and waving his arms, there's trouble in the dressing room.

A manager who gets into that position will then be petrified of taking certain players off because he's scared of the reaction. The players have the power then. Ferguson was the best. Have you ever seen a player ranting and raving at him after coming off?

I was at one club earlier in my career where a teammate used to go mad if he was substituted. He would shake his head, blank the manager and kick the Lucozade bottles as he walked back into the dressing room. It was embarrassing, but it should never have got to that stage.

I was the man who would often come on for him. On top of my salary, I would get £500 for being on the bench and £2,000 (20% of my weekly salary) extra if I came on as sub, good money for a young lad. Yet the hysterics thrown by that player meant he usually stayed on, no matter how badly he was performing. I thought the guy was a selfish prick and so did others, but the manager was petrified of him.

That gaffer was a very good coach, but not a great

manager. And there's a huge difference. He was scared of two or three others in the team who regularly threw tantrums. The coach – who managed at the very highest level – eventually lost his job and was replaced by a hard man with a reputation for not suffering fools gladly. He changed the situation overnight.

We lost a home game unexpectedly. The sulky player was subbed and the fans booed him, so he reacted by making a gesture back. We expected the new manager to read the riot act to us. Instead, he kept us waiting in the dressing room in wet kit for half an hour. Then the kitman came in and told us to shower. We showered and waited as the manager did the media and had a glass of wine with the visiting boss. It was an hour after the game and we sat impatiently in our club suits until the manager came in and, far from being angry, said: 'I'm ever so sorry for keeping you waiting, lads. As I have a few things to say to you. I'll tell you what, rather than do it now why don't you all come in at nine in the morning and we can have a chat then?'

We were gutted. Lads lived an average of ninety minutes away from the training ground. They valued their Saturday nights with their teammates, girlfriends or families. Not only did we realise that he wasn't to be messed with, more soberingly perhaps, we saw that he was clever too.

Next morning, the gaffer came in and asked for a private word with the prima donna in front of all of us. Ten seconds later, the boss came back into the room and said: 'Sorry about that, lads. Just had to deal with him. He won't be playing for me again.'

Then the new manager sat down and said his piece. We

knew he wasn't to be messed with and he never had to assert his authority in that way again.

A good manager also balances his discipline – or he gets his message across with humour. A gaffer once told me that I was like his wife, who couldn't decide which type of knickers to wear each morning. He said that he never knew what he was going to get with her and he felt the same with me when I played for him – his way of saying that I needed to be more consistent.

If he only rants and raves then players soon switch off, sometimes with comic consequences. I saw a manager go crazy and punch the dressing room wall, putting a hole into it, for which the home club sent ours a bill.

Our current manager has been composed while here, but a story has followed him from a previous club. He went apeshit in the dressing room after a defeat, but continued to shower and dress as he sounded off. He's a track-suited manager who gets changed with the lads, probably to suggest we are all in it together. He was ranting and raving as he put his shirt on, saying: 'You lot think I don't have a clue what's going on don't you? You think that I don't know my arse from my elbow. Well you're wrong.' As he said that, he put his socks on. One was red, the other blue – and they definitely weren't 'ironic' socks, but odd socks. That's what you do when you have too much going on in your head.

In better times, after a good Saturday away win, our manager said: 'I don't want to see you until Thursday, you've earned a break.' We loved him for that and temporarily at least wanted to win every game for him. No chance of a manager 'losing a dressing room', whatever that means, if he uses that carrot-and-stick approach.

But it's all about results. Fans are only really bothered about results. Everything else comes second. Fans aren't overly bothered if the club is in serious debt and they're not too concerned if their club is owned by a convicted war criminal or despot, as long as their team wins.

Look at the turnaround by Newcastle fans over their owner Mike Ashley. They went from drinking with him in pubs, to slating him and wanting him out, to thinking that he wasn't so bad again after results improved.

Results change everything in football. When you're winning the mood around any club is great, people feel confident and sing in the corridors.

When you're losing, managers become grumpy and pass on the pressure to their players, they arrange friendly matches or put on extra training sessions. They don't make you any better a player, but they might bring your mind into focus.

A manager will be properly judged only when he's left a club. Players may realise that he was better than they thought; they may be more honest with themselves too and admit that they blamed others when they were at fault themselves.

But there are plenty of bluffers about. You see them coming alive when the television cameras start rolling. I've heard a manager tell the media that he's worked his players really hard all week, when actually he wasn't even at the training ground. Seen a manager take the praise for the improved form of a player by saying that he's had a quiet word with the player. If it was a quiet word in private, why make it public? I've watched a manager say that his side have been doing this or that in training when they haven't been seen at the training ground all week.

There are tactical bluffers too. One told us that 'this team likes to defend behind the ball'. There were sniggers when a player replied: 'Well, they're hardly going to defend in front of it are they?'

There are managers who take the credit for a win when it has been the first-team coach who made the decision which has changed a game. I've seen first-team coaches who are far smarter than the manager in so many ways, but are useless when it comes to the media. Remember Brian Kidd at Manchester United? Great coach, poor manager when he moved to Blackburn, because his lack of media skills left him exposed.

Coaches like Kidd always had the advantage that they were top-level players. That buys respect from players from the start, but it's not unconditional. Everyone knows the story of Glenn Hoddle and Graeme Souness on the training ground – top players in their day, but their day wasn't twenty years after they retired, and lads who trained with them grew frustrated. We had one former player turned manager who continued to train with us, which was fine because he was still in his mid-30s. And we had one manager who would usually join in with training, for the fun part at the end. When he started taking part in five or six a-sides though, it was like being a man down. He no longer had the pace and speed of thought that he'd once boasted.

People say that Arsène Wenger and José Mourinho, two of the most successful coaches in the modern game, never played football. They did. They may have only played to second division level in their countries but they were full-time footballers. They would have been even better managers had they played at the top level, though they did get an early start on their coaching badges.

They knew the game, the way a dressing room works, they didn't come into management blind. Anyone can buy a coaching manual and put a session on, but it's not enough.

A manager may have to deal with a player who is going through a divorce but wants it to remain private, a player who has a persistent injury which isn't clearing up and could end his career. There's an emotional side to management which requires considerably sensitivity.

I've had managers who have lost us games by building up the opposition too much so that we went out there shitting ourselves. They weren't as good as they'd told us.

Conversely, I've seen managers underestimate the opposition, tactical mistakes which cost the team dearly. I played against Cristiano Ronaldo when he was at Manchester United. He'd not been in England long and our manager told us that he was over-rated and one-footed. He went for the 'let him know he's come to XX' by 'letting him know you're here' cliché. Most of our players couldn't get near him to let him know about their presence, and those who did got skinned by his quick feet (both of them) and his speed. The manager got it badly wrong, as he did when he told us that a team lower down in the league were there for the taking. The implication was clear, that they weren't very good. Except they were, or at least their two central midfielders were. They were superior to our players in the same position and one of them soon proved how good he was by getting a move to one of the best teams. We lost 2–0.

THE SECRET PLAYER

Managers desperately want to get certain players in the team, be it a big signing they've made or a star player. Sometimes they want to get two players who play in the same position and one will be deployed out of position. To accommodate a new signing, I was once played out wide, where I'm nowhere near the player I am in my best central position. I'd been playing well and he didn't want to drop me. He should have dropped me, rather than try and keep me happy. It was a fudge and the other players knew it.

Those sorts of decisions can affect your confidence in a boss. One gaffer, like our current manager, had an eye for the ladies, so he created opportunities to pick up women. Every away game involved an overnight stop in the city where we were playing, which wasn't necessary, especially as some of the away matches were only an hour's journey. The gaffer and his staff just wanted a night out. We'd get to the hotel around six on a Friday, have a meal and the players would be packed off to their rooms and bed while the manager and his staff would hit the bar. If he had a woman lined up then she'd come to the hotel.

Next morning at breakfast it would be obvious the staff were hung-over. They wouldn't boast about their conquests, but the players would get wind of what had gone on after a physio blabbed. As when the manager and his staff went out in a city close to where we were playing the next day. They paid £10 to get in a bar and left because it wasn't any good. They walked down the street and paid £10 to get in another bar which looked better. It was the same bar, different entrance. The players hammered the staff for that. Drinking the night before a game is normal for English managers, unheard of for foreign bosses I've worked under.

There's some resentment amongst the players about this 'don't do as I do' situation – and the foreign lads are absolutely baffled that their boss drinks alcohol before matches – though granted the staff don't have to play for ninety-plus hard minutes.

An overly social manager can create bad feeling. The ladies' man made the most of it after one of our lads chatted up a beautiful Scandinavian girl on a pre-season tour and was making progress . . . until the manager stepped in between them and told the player it was past his bed time. Then he continued the chatting up and spent the night with the gorgeous blonde. I saw the same manager try it on with the stunning wife of one player. She wasn't having any of it.

Socialising, with his staff or various women, was an important part of camaraderie for that manager. Women, fast cars and money dominate talk in dressing rooms – and anything that goes with that.

A manager's first-team coach is also a key figure. Like our current one, they are almost always former players. A coach takes the training sessions and is the conduit between players and the gaffer – every boss I've ever had is called 'gaffer' and I still call them gaffer when I meet them years later, even if they are out with their wife. The coach is the boss's eyes and ears and everything he sees will go back to the boss. If a player says something to the coach then it will get back to the manager. Some players may not have the balls to go direct to the manager and may say something to the coach instead.

'What the fuck did he take me off for on Saturday?'

That goes back as: 'X is not happy that he was taken off on Saturday.'

Or a coach will mark a player's card.

'Listen,' he'll say. 'The boss isn't happy with you. He knows that you were out drinking last night, someone spotted you and he's not happy.'

So you have to be careful what you tell a coach – or anyone who works for the manager. I once told the club doctor that I felt depressed. I told him in confidence and I know it got back to my manager, who, to help him do his job, is going to try and find out as much as possible about his players. I thought that the doctor's betrayal of my confidences was deeply unprofessional.

I'm not sure any psychiatrist could sort out some managers' superstitions. We arrived at one away game too early and the gaffer said to the coach driver, 'Just pull over here for twenty minutes.' So a coach full of Premier League footballers sat in a lay-by a mile from the ground passing the time. We won 2–0.

For the next away match, the manager said: 'I want to make sure that we are in a lay-by a mile from the ground at 12.30.' The coach driver looked confused, but did what he was told. We left the hotel early and the coach stopped in the middle of nowhere for half an hour. We thought the manager was crazy . . . but we won again! The traffic was so bad at the next game in London that we didn't have time to stop. We drew.

A lot of managers will keep their team training the same way if they win a match, or they will 'reward' players by taking out the more unpopular aspects of being a footballer. Ice baths were all but compulsory at one club because the fitness coach insisted on their beneficial effects, but, after one away win, the gaffer said, 'The lads don't need an ice bath today, they've done well.' The fitness man was going crazy, but the gaffer just laughed it off. The players put their fingers up to the fitness coach.

Win, and you can have a beer on the coach home. I've even seen players smoke a few fags on the bus home after a victory, opening the skylight and standing on the seat. There was a divider halfway. More people smoke in football than you'd think, though it's more occasional. I don't know of any twenty a day players.

Lose and it's not even a good idea to walk around the city where your team play in the afternoon.

After some patchy results, we win convincingly at home. The replacement, on for the first time, though I'm not subbed, scores – well, he would do, wouldn't he? And he wheels away into the crowd, celebrating his first goal like crazy – he's allowed that one. Some players are shameless in their courting of fans' adulation. I've played with lads who will go to the toilet when the rest of us run out for the warm up. Then they'll come out a minute later clapping everyone and milking applause, the big 'look at me'. That doesn't go down well with the other players.

Every player secretly wants to be idolised by the fans. Two or three usually are at any club, with the jury out on a further four or five. Another two or three will be scapegoats who get blamed for everything. That's just how it is.

There are players who know how to milk a song. They'll spend longer than the rest signing autographs, for example. Or stay until they're the last one on the bus. One colleague, who was playing well at the time, waited to leave the bus last at a game where a lot of our fans were waiting so that he could bask in the applause and get his thirty seconds of love.

As the other players disembarked and went straight in the ground, he pretended to look under the seat, as if he'd lost something. I knew what his game was, so I also pretended to look under the seat, because I knew it would wind him up. The coach driver shouted to us both: 'Come on, boys, the police want to move me on.' Which was understandable as we were outside the main entrance to the stadium.

So determined was he to be last that I buckled first and left the coach, where I got a decent cheer. When I walked into the changing room the manager wasn't pleased and asked where the fuck I'd been.

'And where's that other idiot?' he continued. Then we heard more cheering; it was the other player getting the applause that he was so desperate for.

Another player did a solo lap of honour after every single game, a jog around as if every game was the last match of the season. The fans loved him for it. He felt that he was applauding the people who paid his wages and I can see his point, but I don't agree with it. I felt that was disrespectful to the rest of the team. If we all did a lap of honour or went to applaud the home end like they do in Germany then I'd be fine with that, but isn't football supposed to be a team game?

SEPTEMBER

The manager would be talking to us after the game and one of the players would pipe up: 'Give it half an hour gaffer so that X can get his applause and then hear you too.' Everyone enjoyed that one.

But jealousy came into it. The player was so professional that you couldn't pick holes in him or his game. And nobody likes someone who is perfect. There was a very slight chink in his armour, however.

His wife, a lovely looking girl and a lovely person, used to see a different footballer who was a bit of a lad. It was well before she met her husband, but to undermine hubby's goody-two-shoes image, the former boyfriend used to tell people that she was wild in bed, into S&M, the lot. People only half believed him, but it made you look at his wife in a different light.

Some fans will wait for you after the game. Usually they want an autograph or a small chat. Fine, but if things are not going well they might have a go. At a rival club, a fan told the star striker that he was a waste of space as he got in his car.

'Why don't you fuck off back to your council estate?' replied the angry player. Then he got in his Bentley and drove off.

By the end of September the league starts to take shape. We've won two, drawn two and lost two and we're 13th. That's passable. Had we lost one more game, for the first time you might think 'we're struggling here'. It might be down to fitness: you think you've had a good pre-season and done all the sports science stuff, the body fat indexes and the heart monitors, but you realise that the other teams are still fitter. That's why you get some freak results at the start of the season. If the fans see you are struggling too then they might think the same and start turning against the players, the manager or those in charge of the club – all just six weeks after the most optimistic point of the season. You'd know something was definitely amiss – usually the writing is on the wall – if the club owner comes down to the training ground. He'll turn up in his Rolls-Royce and pretend that everything is fine, but he's there to keep an eye on things because he hasn't got confidence about what's going on at the training ground.

The current owner finds the dressing room an intimidating place. He gets enough grief off fans because the club doesn't win the treble every season, so he doesn't bother us that much. I think that stems back to when he was critical of the players last season and, when he next saw us, one of the players told him matter-of-factly that his comments helped nobody. He's a good man who had made his millions through hard work.

Absentee owners are the best owners. Owners think they are managers; I've never met one who doesn't. They'll say 'how come you're not picking X or I'm surprised that you didn't play X?' Managers will bow down to them a lot of the time and do as the owners say.

At one club, the owner really got the hump with the players because results were poor. He cut the quality of the food at the training ground, told us to buy our own protein drinks and his attitude was: 'I pay you a fortune and you're failing me.'

A club owner would have the ear of a senior player or the kitman – a mole, who he would get information from. It might be innocent stuff, to ask how a certain player has settled in. If he's paid £6 million for someone, then he's entitled to know as much about his expensive acquisition as possible.

Players will brown-nose the owner too – he's the man ultimately responsible for saying 'yes' or 'no' when they want a new contract. They'll be all sweetness and light with the owner's (inevitably younger) wife too, though maybe shagging her in an executive box like one lad did after one drunken trophy celebration wasn't the brightest idea. I don't think the owner found out about that.

I keep my distance from owners, keep myself to myself and I'm polite when I see them. When it comes to owners, I have fond memories of one who, shall we say, liked a glass of wine. At one game, he sat next to the manager in the stand, where he said: 'I can't understand why the crowd are being like this, we're playing well and have scored twice.' To which the manager replied: 'It's the other team who have scored. We're in our away strip today.'

The manager could hardly talk. Earlier in his career, he handed in the team sheet at one of the biggest clubs in the country. He saw the opponents' team, which was full of big name internationals, some of whom he's been told were out. He walked back to the dressing room going 'Fuck!'. Except he walked into the home, not the away team dressing room where he was supposed to go. All the big name players saw him overcome by nerves. But, incredibly, his side won that day.

The always suitably refreshed owner? He once pulled me to one side and said:

'Well done X, you did well at the weekend.'

'Thanks,' I replied, not having the heart, or maybe the balls, to tell him that I'd been out injured for three weeks.

October

October – no time for excuses any more, the month it can all go wrong, when the sacking season starts. And don't think that only applies to struggling clubs. Roberto Di Matteo was sacked six months after winning the Champions League Trophy. A manager might get away with talking about the team or players needing time to gel in September, but not in October.

The weather starts to turn, leaves clutter the pristine training-ground pitches and the sun decides it's going to disappear for six months. Or that's what any foreign players will tell you, ignoring the fact that there are some beautiful sunny autumn and winter days.

Pre-season is a distant memory and, unlike in January and February where players say 'you can almost see the beach' all you can see in October is the long, hard season in front of you. Games come thick and fast, two matches a week in league and cup. You're always knackered, always sore from the knocks you pick up and you always feel that you need a good sleep. You're either preparing for a game or recovering from one.

I'm not alone among footballers in suffering from insomnia after a midweek game. My mind races after a match, replaying incidents, the adrenaline still in my system, and it's often 4 or 5 a.m. before I can sleep after an away match. Then we have to be up at seven or eight. That's why we feel shattered.

There is no full training on a Thursday, replaced by a recovery session. I think they're a waste of time. Your recovery starts after a match. Hang around any stadium and you'll often see the players come back out onto the pitch for a warm down. If you've won, then you've done your job and you pay as little attention as possible. Players will be talking about what's happening that night.

The fitness coach will be moaning and he might even get back-up from the manager, that's if the manager hasn't got the hump and ordered us all straight back on the bus after a defeat. It all depends on the result.

Fitness coaches are not popular. One player at our club calls the head fitness coach 'clipboard' because he's always walking around with a clipboard. He takes the piss because of the number of letters after his name, the result of numerous qualifications.

'Oi, Clipboard,' he'll shout, 'How many degrees you got this week? I bet you've still not had a shag.'

Some fitness gurus try to justify their position and job, but if you've got a tired mind – like after a defeat – then you'll have tired legs.

The recovery session the day after is six laps of a training pitch in a gentle jog, plus some stretching. Waste of time.

I've done every recovery session: flotation tanks, ice baths and walking into freezers of different temperatures. They're not for me. If you've missed an open goal with the crowd booing you, no recovery session will help.

No recovery session prevents the aches and pains, the tiredness. I feel dead the day after a game.

This season's fixture list has thrown up the first derby match of the season in October. The city has been looking forward to this for months, but derbies don't mean as much to the players as the supporters, who have their own, different rivalries at work and in the pub to act out.

Players prepare the same for every game and derbies are no different. Fans are far more up for some games than others, but players can't afford the same highs and lows in their preparation.

Fans noticeably start to change their behaviour in the week before the derby. A trip to the supermarket with your family will see more people coming up to you.

'I'm sorry to interrupt your shopping with your family,' they'll say, doing it anyway, 'but good luck in sticking it up those bastards at the weekend.'

The media, led by Sky TV, search for spoiling stories. It's a dream for them if someone from either side says something negative about a person from the other team. But the media can spoil some games because they build them up, adding too much pressure and tension. Expectations can be so high that they are impossible to meet. They might say that there are always goals when Liverpool plays Everton, implying that goals are the key to a good game. Footballers see it differently. There is such a thing as a great 0–0 draw, where the defence has kept a clean sheet at a difficult away ground.

The atmosphere is clearly different for a derby game. When we run out onto the pitch it hits us: the noise level louder than usual, a packed stadium and away end, with fans singing back and forward at each other. I love all that, it shows how much the game means to fans and I really want to do well for them, but my attitude is the same as the previous week, also my preparation. It has to be. If you start to let emotion into your thought process then you are going to become overwrought and make irrational decisions. I'm sure I'd be a hero forever with some fans if I punched the opposing player they really hate, but I'd rather have a decent career than infamy and free pints for life in a city's pubs.

Derby days are the loudest though songs from the crowd can stir up jealousy among players when some have their names sung over and again, while others don't have their name sung at all.

Some poor players have their name sung all the time because they have a good song about them. They become cult heroes only because of their songs. Certain songs grate, especially that 'Walking in a XXXX wonderland.' That 'Who Ar Ya?' irritates me as well.

One thing does improve in a derby. Players who have previously been barracked will be given a match's grace. There's no time for turning on your own in a derby, you keep it in the family and supporters don't want to be shown up abusing their own players. Today tackles are flying in a touch more.

We go ahead and, cringingly, the scorer, departing from his usual muted raised arm celebration for the derby, kisses the badge and waves to the crowd to get them going. Too theatrical and forced for my taste, but the fans like it. To them, it shows that the player is passionate about the club and they'll claim there are not enough passionate players about 'like there used to be'. But he's just buying some cheap popularity.

Some players don't need to court the crowd because they are already treated like a god. I played with one lad who was adored. He'd scored some key goals for his club and been there for a long time as the club went through a lot of ups and downs. He could have left at various stages, but chose to stay and the fans loved him for it. He was a good player, not a great one and as charismatic off the field as he was wearing the shirt.

What the fans didn't know was that he'd toss it off at the training ground midweek, throwing bombs all over the shop. 'Throwing bombs' is a term players use for a troublemaker, the player who has power and abuses it. He might be half-hearted in training, he might go up to a group of three or four players and say to one of them: 'I can't believe the gaffer took you off at the weekend, he's losing it.' He undermines because he can, the manager's biggest nightmare because he's so popular with fans that the manager can't win. Drop him or sell him and he'll be slaughtered, so the manager's best bet is to try and indulge him.

This player's confidence will also come from knowing that he's the best paid man in the dressing room. Money is a taboo subject in the dressing room because a player can be earning ten times what his teammate sitting next to him is on. We don't talk about it, we just know – or we have a very good idea – about who is on what. Players may let something slip after a beer or during contract negotiations, the media will chip in with what they know and our agents are always ready to let us know that someone other than their clients is raking it in.

I wouldn't expect you to have any sympathy for footballers and their seven-figure salaries, but money brings serious problems outside the dressing room.

Here's why. Most footballers come from poor backgrounds. They dream of wealth as a solution to all their problems, yet it often becomes their biggest. Dodgy agents, financial advisors, hangers on and women – I've seen them all do damage to rich young men.

Some don't help themselves. They squander money on flash cars and boob jobs for their wives. Someone always wants to have the best car in the car park and will pay through the nose for that dubious 'privilege'. There are footballers who think your car equates to your status in the team. Even top of the range, wildly expensive motors are not out of bounds to practical jokers. Last week, a young pro came in his new black car, his first nice motor, but it did look like a baby hearse. Three hours later, someone had written 'Funeral Directors' along the side in spray snow. Don't ask me why someone had spray snow in October.

I've driven home from training with: 'I shag fifteen-year-olds' and 'I like cock' etched in dirt on the side of my car without me knowing it. Not sure what my grandma made of that one when I drove away from her house after a visit.

A car is essential. The training ground is out in the sticks and motorbikes are as off limits for players as skiing holidays and white water rafting.

Players pay over-the-top money for designer clothes they seldom wear and have four-figure monthly phone bills. Nobody teaches a young footballer what to do with their money. The clubs don't really care because it's not their responsibility, while the PFA are well intentioned – but intervene usually only when something goes wrong. A player will often go to them when it's too late.

You don't get a second chance to earn money when you're a footballer – you basically have two or three contracts when you can earn big bucks because when you're eighteen you're on relative peanuts.

Agents are often in with financial advisors and take cuts off the rich clients they steer towards them and the products they buy. They don't always have the best interests of their client at heart and there are plenty of agents who pretend to be best mates with their clients . . . until the money stops.

Footballers don't always help themselves because they don't listen and often prefer to give it the big one about what they earn in the dressing room. They don't go around saying: 'I earn XXX' – it's more subtle than that. They express their wealth in the cars they buy or their women express it by boasting about their clothes and houses.

Some girls marry for love, but I've heard some horror stories about gold-diggers. One told her husband, a Premier League star and full international, that she wanted a divorce two weeks after he announced he was retiring. She took him to the cleaners.

Young professionals can get stung by the fairer sex. They are usually with one of two types of girls. Some pair up with their childhood sweetheart. She might be the best-looking girl on the estate. Think Coleen Rooney. She knew Wayne was going to be something and he knew she was the best girl around.

Or a girl they've met since they've become properly famous, a girl who wouldn't look twice at them if they were not rich, athletic and famous. There are hidden dangers here. The lads go for looks, little more. It's hard for them to resist some of the beautiful girls who suddenly become available to them – and those beautiful girls will try hard to pin them down as their boyfriends and become accustomed to a life of absolute luxury. They'll have their teeth and tits done, they'll spend a fortune being ladies who lunch, but they'll always be aspiring to something more.

I was an apprentice when I met my wife. She was working full-time. She was sensible then and sensible now. When I made it, when the money really started coming in after I broke into the first team, her attitude was: 'We might only have five or six years so don't squander it.' She's been really cautious any time we've spent a lot of money, asking, 'Do we really need this?' Sometimes I've told her to relax, that I'm earning a lot, a lot more than the man in the street and we can afford a second home in the sun. And we can. But mostly I have been very grateful for her level-headedness. There are women who would happily work their way through their man's fortune and treat money without the respect it deserves. Just as there are footballers perfectly capable of frittering away their money without any assistance.

That money is naturally a source of great envy. I am making a living doing what thousands would love to do and while some people are pleased for you, others definitely aren't.

There is some envy from local players who didn't make it, but it is more likely to come from their parents. The type who genuinely thought that their son was going to be a top footballer and became so obsessed with that enticing prospect that they poured all their time into watching him as an investment towards future riches. An investment which didn't pay off. One came up to me last week: 'Are you still getting stick off the crowd?' he asked. The person had not spoken to me for two years; I've barely had any stick off the crowd, but for some reason his first point to me, before he could even comment on the weather, was a negative. Good news doesn't make headlines in football, bad news does.

Away from you, the parents will say: 'That could have been my son if it wasn't for injury,' or 'He wasn't even the best player in the team.' To your face, someone might say: 'It's alright for someone with your money' or, 'What did you buy that car for? If I had your money I would have bought an X.' People are obsessed with how much money you earn. They don't ask you personally how much you earn, but they ask people close to you. My uncle took great pride in massively inflating my earnings when questioned. I've no idea why.

And then there's the accusation that 'You've gone all big time.' I was called that by a local man who showed no interest in me at all until I was an established Premier League player. Then he knocked at my parents' house. He wanted to know if I'd go into business with him. Something about water purification taps for kitchens. He'd do the work, I'd put the money up. He gave my parents his number, was very insistent. I called him. I felt like saying: 'Don't ever go to my parents' house again,' but instead had to listen to his drivel about how he'd make us millions. He was unemployed at the time, and with a chequered history from where I grew up. He simply saw me as a meal ticket out of his shit life. I said thanks but no thanks, lying that I had too much on. That made me a 'big timer who'd turned his back on his roots' – despite me being firmly in touch with my roots. I couldn't defend myself, but my mates did. I'd like to think that my reputation held intact. Truth is, though, some footballers are 'big time', that is, arrogant. They believe their own hype, they're not nice people. I'm not one of them.

You can't say yes to everything, to be all things to all people who want your time. Or money.

Nor is envy restricted to strangers. Family can think you should give more of your cash to them, buying them more lavish Christmas presents because they've read in the paper that you earn X a week. They don't realise that you don't earn the published figure, that you are not paid by the week and that even if you did your salary is a lot, lot less after tax and agent commissions. You usually end up with half of it. Most footballers learn the difference between gross and net when they look with horror at how much tax they've paid on their salary slip.

I look after my parents at Christmas, but I know my brothers expect more from me – not that they'd ever tell me. Sad, isn't it?

One lad bought his parents a house so they could move out of the council house they rented. Then his wife got the hump because he didn't buy her parents a house too. Money is a minefield.

I know players who have been sensible and invested wisely in multiple properties, pensions, stocks and shares. And I know others who once cost millions and now sign on with nothing to show for their career but memories. They're the type who thought they were richer than they were and that it would never end. They thought they were different from other people and didn't have to worry about the future because of the adulation they received in the present. Some of them earned serious money and some still do – there's a player I know on £40,000 a week and has been for eight years. I'd be stunned if he has any left five years after he's finished because he's wasted millions on fast cars and fast women and he has court orders to pay for his three different children with three different women. His 'mates' were salesmen from the luxury car showroom who have made thousands from him, yet the player can't see it.

People like him have made the correct decisions in the game to get to where they are. They're not stupid. They train hard and eat well. They are good professionals on the pitch. Off it, it's a completely different matter.

There's a subtle pressure in the dressing room to spend your money to conform to the group norm. There's also a lot of spare time to spend all that money on things you don't need.

At least this October, our manager doesn't look like he's going to be sacked, especially not after the fillip of our derby win. It wasn't pleasant to watch when it happened to me at another club. Results were not going well, the chairman started showing up at the training ground more often and training started lasting longer, with more double sessions. The injured players were told to get in earlier.

The manager's personality changed and you could see that he was feeling the pressure. He stopped being bubbly and became irritable. And, after one home defeat to one of the few teams below us in the league, you could see that he gave up. Back in the dressing room, he looked resigned and said: 'I've said enough to you lot and you didn't listen to me. There's not much more that I can do. You've let me down big time, you've let yourselves and your families down too. I hope you feel good about yourselves.'

He was right. We had let him down.

He never said as much, but he knew that he was going to be sacked and started going through the motions.

Three days later, we heard the news that he'd been dismissed. He didn't tell us, the chairman did, when he came to the dressing room after training and explained that a change needed to be made, that things needed to improve and that the new manager would be joining in the next few days. In the meantime, the manager's former assistant would take charge of the preparation for the following weekend's game.

Two things weren't standard there. One, players often find out about sackings through the media. Two, the assistant is often dismissed with the manager and one of the fitness coaches. They'll travel from club to club together.

Most of the players texted or rang the outgoing manager to say that they were sorry and wished him well for the future. He replied with a text saying: 'No problem. Keep going.' No matter how he was feeling, he couldn't afford to burn his bridges with players he might end up working with again.

Players are not always so careful. If they don't like or rate the manager, they see no point pretending otherwise. One sacked manager who'd been there five years held a leaving party at his house. Only four players turned up, a poor show. At another club, the manager gave a grand leaving speech, thanking us for all our efforts. I didn't think that was a good idea. I can see why he wanted to do it, but it seemed wasted to save his best speech until he was no longer in the job.

After the October sacking, the assistant took charge on a temporary basis. We were fine with that. We all knew him and he was keen to be everyone's friend. The players were happy to be his friend, for him to be appointed full-time, because they knew him.

That was unlikely, because he didn't have the experience of the outgoing manager, but he'd identified a few areas which could be improved and he wasn't under the same pressure as the previous coach, the pressure which had made the training ground so miserable. That alone lifted the mood, though much of the pressure was transferred to the players. The fans were hardly going to boo a caretaker who'd been in the job five minutes were they?

All the time speculation swirled round about his replacement. I was filled with dread at some names being linked to the job and thought: 'Please don't let it be him' about one candidate who'd sold me from a previous club.

Occasionally, the caretaker manager will attempt to stamp his authority on the job, his new status going straight to his head. Once he changed his tracksuit for a suit, he started saying in the press that he wanted the job and that he knew how to fix things. He wasted no time in parking his car in the manager's spot. He even started talking differently as if he was a bit posher than he actually was! He also dropped three players who'd been playing OK. We couldn't take him seriously. He didn't get the job permanently and it was a bit embarrassing for him to return to his tracksuit as the youth team coach a few weeks later.

The caretaker will rarely get the job permanently. This is risky and familiarity can quickly lead to contempt. He has to go from being matey and appearing to be a confidante of the players to being the one who dishes out the discipline.

While there is uncertainty between managers, one of the few cornerstones of the dressing room is the kitman. A manager can be sacked, his assistant and any others he has brought in, the lead fitness coach for example, but the kitman is never sacked.

Kitmen often stay until they retire and their job doesn't just entail washing clothes. At a Premier League club they'll have a couple of assistants to help them do that. The greatest ability that any kitman can have is to keep his mouth shut. He sees and hears everything, so he has to be trusted not to say anything. He needs to be quick-witted too. If he's not then he'd get bullied. And a lot of that goes on in football.

While the manager tries his best to support players, he's got too much on his plate to care for the personal welfare of every individual. The kitman steps in. A player may arrive from France or Brazil. He doesn't know anyone and can't speak English. The kitman will do his best to make him feel at home. The best one I've worked with was full of wisecracks. He would destroy players from Liverpool in a false Scouse accent, he would learn a couple of words of any language of any new player. You wouldn't believe what difference it can make to a new French player sat alone in a dressing room when the kitman says: 'Bonjour. Je m'appelle John et j'ai deux lapins et un chat,' in a terrible accent.

The same kitman would invite every new player for a meal with his family. It was a simple, yet superb gesture. He earned £22,000 a year and lived in a normal house in a working-class part of the city. The players would tap his address into the sat navs of their £60,000 cars and park on the street outside his house. His wife would make a Sunday roast or similar. The foreign players loved that touch of normality. Though one didn't, and turned down the offer. The knobhead. We didn't like anyone knocking the kitman back. The same player couldn't be bothered to learn English. It was so obvious that he only came to England for the money. We didn't blame him, but he shouldn't have made it so blatant.

We took our revenge on him by teaching him the wrong words when he wanted to ask for something in his terrible English. He wanted to know the word for butter and bread, which came out as: 'Can I suck your tits?' to a waiter in a pre-match hotel. As he did it, he made the motion of a knife spreading butter on bread.

Other foreign players are taught the wrong words, so you'll hear them saying: 'minging' or not realising how strong 'fuck off' is. As he was politely told that he would have to wait two minutes in the canteen for pasta, a really pleasant Spanish signing replied: 'Oh, fuck off!' to the canteen girl. He had no idea how insulting it was until the kitman shouted: 'Wooah, don't speak to a lady like that.'

That kitman was a legend. He was a big fella and would stand behind the (much smaller) manager like his minder if he ever got into a confrontation with the fourth official or a rival manager.

The kitman will bollock players for being lazy with their kits like a strict school teacher. He'll be the butt of the jokes but will give it back. He'll be the social convenor, a 'vibesman' if that doesn't sound ridiculous, someone the players can ask for advice – often about the most simple of things as they adjust to life in their new country.

'Have you heard this, lads? He wants to know how to turn the lights off in his new home at night!' It wasn't true, the player had a genuine problem with his lights at home (probably something like a bulb needed changing), but it got a laugh and even the player, in his faltering English, had to laugh.

Losing a manager by 'mutual consent' (is that like saying it was 'mutual' when a girl ends a relationship?) changes the mood, but it doesn't change results. Chairmen think it does and there is anecdotal evidence and clear examples of short-term improvements after changes. Professional managers used to be in their jobs for an average of three years, now it's fourteen months, but the hard statistics prove that, long-term, change is not always good. They prove that changing a manager is often more harmful to a team's performance than doing nothing. At one of my clubs, they got rid of an experienced boss just two months into the season. He'd had to face a tough run of fixtures and do so without several key players. 'No win in six' or 'fighting relegation already' was trotted out in the press, but they didn't mention the fixture list, which he had no control over, or the serious injuries. I say serious, because some were anything but.

When the boss was dismissed, sorry, left by mutual consent, some of the injured players made the most remarkable of recoveries in a short space of time – which would have helped our departing manager if the miracle had occurred sooner.

A new boss needs to be respected from the start. He'll bring an assistant and a fitness man and they'll almost always say that the team they've taken over are not fit enough.

Players are suspicious, because they'll be expecting a wave of new signings to follow and will be worried about their own future. They will also raise their game. The injured players knew that they would mean nothing to the incoming manager and wanted to make a good impression. And players do feign injuries, as I've said earlier, for a variety of reasons, as well as concealing them.

My last team had just been promoted to the Premier League, triggering a large bonus of around £1 million into the players' pool. It would be divided according to appearances.

My groin injury was a nightmare, but I worked out that each game was worth £7,000 on top of my normal wages. We had a few matches left and so I decided to keep quiet about it. I couldn't tell the physio or club doctor because they are in cahoots with the manager. I know my body and decided to play through the pain, so I strapped myself up and hammered the ibuprofen. I got through the game and I took the money. Do I regret it? No.

Footballers, like most in society, put themselves first. Sad, but true. I wouldn't have played in an FA Cup final under the same conditions, but it wasn't a Cup final.

There's not a player who has been completely honest about his fitness. It usually takes the form of dragging your recovery out longer than you need. A player might not fancy a certain game, most often an international match. So he tells his international manager that he has a dodgy hamstring or calf. The clubs encourage it – they'd rather a player rested up for a week.

Fans might be disgusted that a player doesn't want to play for his country, but your loyalty is first and foremost to the club which pays your wages. The excuses don't just apply in international football. I know a top international who is idolised by fans, but he just didn't fancy an FA Cup away match at a fourth division team in January. So he said he had a hamstring problem. The manager knew what was going on, but the player was the biggest personality at the club and the manager turned a blind eye and indulged him. The other players weren't impressed, especially when their team coach left the day before the game and they saw the injured player doing sprints with one of the physios. They didn't like it and rightly saw it as one rule for one.

Not every injury is what it seems either. One player was out for three months after having unconventional intercourse with a girl. Let's just say that a corn cob was transferred from one body to the other and use the phrases 'severe swelling' 'groin issues', 'bloodstream' and 'swollen glands'.

Another player, a goalkeeper, went to warm up before a Premier League game. He ignored the large 'Please Keep Out of the Goal Mouth Area' notice and went over on his ankle in the warm up on the roughest part of the pitch.

He sprained his ankle badly and the manager had a go at the groundsman, who correctly pointed out the sign and explained that's why there was a portable goal twenty yards to the left of the goal. The manager had to back down and the reserve goalie played.

At another club, some of the lads had a round of golf two days before a match. That's not allowed because players should save their legs rather than walk 6,000 yards. They came up with the bright idea of hiring a buggy. They played for money and one player hit a shot into the rough, prompting the others to laugh so much that the buggy went into a bunker and rolled over. The driver dislocated his shoulder and had to come clean to the manager, not least because an ambulance was called to the golf course so there was no hiding the incident.

Another player had a fight on a night out in his home city after one game and fractured his cheekbone. He called the physio the next morning and told him that he'd 'had a whack at the end of game on Saturday'. The physio told him to come in early the next day to have a look. He was X-rayed and told that he'd fractured his cheekbone. He was out for six weeks and nobody else knows how he got the injury to this day.

Some players, mainly younger ones, won't listen to anyone. One teammate, who I'd describe as a talented fool, played five-a-side with his mates. Not only should he not have been playing, but he got sent off during the game and became embroiled in a fight which continued after the match in the car park. The police were called and he was arrested.

The player went to see the manager the next day, where he apologised, not just for playing, but for getting sent off, for getting in a fight, for getting injured and being arrested. Then he capped it all by asking for help. The manager was not happy, but the club stuck by him and supported him in court. Why? Because he was good and that can make all the difference.

Mishaps and pranks are part of being a footballer. If you don't like a prank then don't become a professional footballer. I'm not suggesting that we all fire air guns in training like Ashley Cole, but you have to be able to give it out – and more importantly, take it – in the dressing room.

I once bought some lovely Prada jeans. They were my pride and joy and I wore them to training three days in succession. I was invited to be a guest on *Football Focus* and – guess what – wore the jeans. Unbeknown to me, my teammates were watching me on TV and slaughtering me.

I went into Knightsbridge after the game and visited the Prada store. There, I overheard a girl say to her boyfriend, 'They're the jeans that lad was wearing on *Football Focus*. That's what we've come to buy.' I didn't tell her that I was the lad on *Football Focus*.

The jeans were washed but I wore them to training a few days later. I was injured and had to go in for treatment while the other lads trained. One of the other injured players had a serious drink problem – and this was at a Premier League club. That morning, he disappeared for an hour and came back absolutely smashed. We found out that he'd gone into one of the sponsor's lounges and drunk directly from the optics.

His drinking would ultimately affect his career, but I sat him down and got him a coffee in an attempt to sober him up. He repaid me by cutting up my beloved jeans. I realised when I returned to a full dressing room after treatment. The lads were all sniggering.

The dressing room is a dangerous place. I once bought a can of Deep Heat and sprayed a bit into my teammates' boxer shorts just before they finished training. I'd seen this done before and knew what to expect. Once it kicks in, the pain is excruciating and lasts all day.

We had a big afternoon out planned after training and had a minibus to take us into town. I started to see players scratching their nuts. Then I heard one say: 'I don't know what's wrong, but my balls are on fire. I can't stop itching.'

'I feel like someone has put Deep Heat on my balls,' added another knowledgeably. Then he put his hand inside his boxers and smelled that unmistakeable aroma. I kept my mouth shut. When we got to the restaurant, most of the team rushed into the toilets to throw their boxers away and wash their bollocks with fresh water. They worked out it was me, because I wasn't scratching and was grinning.

Because I looked a little older than I was, the lads used to take the mickey out of me. A waitress approached and asked: 'Could you stand on this chair please, sir?' I obliged and as everyone in the restaurant looked at me, she delivered a cake with 'Happy 50th Birthday' on it. The lads then picked bits off the cake and started throwing it at me. Maybe I deserved it.

And you should never leave your phone on show in the dressing room. We got hold of one phone and changed the number from a girl the player was seeing to the number of a teammate he didn't already have on his phone.

We were in a hotel and started texting the lad – who thought he was getting texts from his girl. The exchanges started innocently enough, but soon got a bit steamy and we asked him to send saucy photos of himself.

When we asked him his nickname, he replied, 'The Dragon. You can unleash me.' That was news to us. We made it clear that she was gagging for it and begged him for a meeting that night. He invited the girl to the team hotel, completely against club rules.

'But what about your teammate who you room with?' we suggested. 'Shouldn't you get another room?'

He duly paid up and the tryst was arranged for room 109 at 10 p.m., where, he promised, 'The Dragon' would be ready and waiting, naked.

At the appointed hour, most of the first-team squad were positioned outside room 109. We covered the spy hole and charged in when he opened the door wearing nothing but an open dressing gown.

The would-be Romeo was devastated and tried to save face, shouting, 'I knew it was you lot!'

The hotel staff grassed to the manager that the player in question had paid for a separate room for a girl. He was fuming and told him that he was being fined a week's wages. The manager was very strict and some of the senior players (and you become a senior player by playing games, not because you are old. You can be a senior player at twenty-four) had to fight the player's corner, explaining that he had to get a single room because his teammate's snoring was really bad. The boss believed it and the fine was dropped. He still has no idea of what went on.

Some pranks would be considered bullying. I got hammered when I was a young pro by some horrible people – horrible on and off the pitch. I gave the ball away in one of my first training sessions with the first team and all I could hear was a load of bigger, older, famous men shouting, 'You're fucking shit', 'What the fuck is he doing playing with us?' and 'Is this your decision, gaffer, or has he won a competition?'

I was traumatised, but it was their way of toughening me up. It was bullying. I'd go out with them socially and my overriding emotion would be fear.

I'd been in the first-team squad two weeks when I returned from the shower after training to see a towel which wasn't my own covering my tracksuit. Everyone was waiting around watching me, even if they were pretending not to.

I lifted the towel to see that my favourite adidas tracksuit had had a run in with a pair of scissors. The tracksuit bottoms were now shorts, so brief that they wouldn't have looked out of place on a gay fetish night. Oh, and the arms had been cut off. So my favourite tracksuit was now a tank top and a pair of trunks. I had three options. Laugh, cry or start throwing punches. I smiled. They made me put it back on so that they could have a good laugh at me, made me drive back to my digs looking like a freak.

The most popular prank involves cutting off the end of a pair of socks with scissors from the treatment room, where someone doesn't realise and pulls them right up their legs. Another lad had a hole cut out of the front of his £50 D&G

boxer shorts. He didn't realise, pulled them on and his bollocks just spilled out. Stupid, immature, but always funny.

I've seen a beautiful Prada coat cut up, countless pairs of jeans wrapped up in physio tape so that they take twenty minutes to untangle, numerous pairs of laces cut on shoes and trainers. I've had mayonnaise poured into my coat pockets and not realised for a few hours until I put my hands in them.

I've seen dustbins emptied into people's cars and heard of all kinds of pranks. At one non-league club where I'm from, the manager had enough with a 'big time' player. So he smeared his own shit between two pieces of bread and laced the sandwich with cucumber, tomato and lettuce to hide the excrement. He passed the player a sandwich and he had swallowed three mouthfuls before he suspected anything was wrong.

Some of my funniest moments as a footballer have been pranks. They've also involved alcohol.

Football and alcohol go hand-in-hand. I got off the bus after my first away trip as a seventeen-year-old and the handles on my kit bag nearly snapped off because the older players had used it for their empty bottles. The captain told me to keep quiet and dispense of the empties discreetly. I did. I'd not even noticed the other players drinking on the four-hour coach trip back. I learned that the manager turned a blind eye if the team had won, but that the players had to be ultra-discreet if they hadn't. Apart from anything, alcohol is illegal on all football coaches. But there are times when what is still a deep-rooted drinking culture can't be ignored.

I played with a lad at a Premier League club who had a serious alcohol problem. He wasn't what I'd call an old school drinker, one who knocked back ten pints in a session with the team. No, the midfielder who scored some crucial goals at the biggest grounds, found himself in a dark place and turned to drink to make himself happier.

He was from a good family, but he couldn't handle alcohol and became a liability after a few drinks. He'd cut peoples' clothes up or start slapping girls' backsides in clubs – then get thrown out.

His dependence soon spiralled out of control and he couldn't come close to being considered for the first team. He was once found asleep on a kid's slide outside a pub when the team coach came to pick him up.

He needed help and he got it; from the football club, his family and Alcoholics Anonymous. In one of his first meetings at AA, he had to stand up and say: 'My name is X and I'm an alcoholic.'

His mentor there told him to ring up all of his teammates and explain that he was an alcoholic. He called me and said: 'Hello mate, it's X here. I'm just calling to say that I'm an alcoholic. I'm getting treatment. I'm in the right place. I hope to be back soon.'

I knew he had issues, was saddened by the phone call and wished him well.

Then he rang the team captain and said the same thing.

'Fuck off, I drink more than you,' replied the captain. 'I'll come down there and drink all of them under the table.' To him it was football banter. The player didn't see the funny side but the captain never relented. The player did come back, but soon fell by the wayside again and out of football.

OCTOBER

If you have a problem in football then you get one chance to get over it. People will bend over backwards to help you, but they won't do it forever. The bottom line is that you are privileged to be a professional footballer and your career is a short one. If you don't make the best of that then you are partly to blame.

Alcohol is a difficult one for managers. Many have come from a generation when all the lads regularly went out together on a session. That happened every week until a decade ago and there would be 'Tuesday clubs' up and down the country – which entailed the players going to the pub after training on Tuesday for a nine-hour bonding binge. With Wednesday usually being the day off in football, the hangovers were over in time for Thursday training. Because most clubs did it, it was not unusual. Remember that the all-conquering Liverpool were just as dedicated drinkers as Man United in the eighties, while some of United's best players were the biggest drinkers like Bryan Robson, Norman Whiteside and Paul McGrath.

Managers don't like drinking now, but they can't control their players 24/7 either. There have been big changes. Non-drinking foreign players were part of the reason, plus higher levels of fitness across the board, yet drinking is still an important part of the camaraderie.

I was at one club where a local boxer had a major contest four days before we had a big game. Boxers often latch on to a club to tap into their support. We all planned to go to London to see him fight, but the manager got wind of it and stopped us. He only changed his mind after we agreed not to drink. We ignored him and all got slaughtered. Unfortunately for us, the bout was live on television and the commentator made several references to us being there – and the cameras showed we were clearly well-oiled.

The boss was livid. He threatened all of us with a week's fine if we didn't win the crucial game on the Sunday. We made sure that we won.

Foreign players are often baffled by the drinking culture, which, admittedly, has changed a lot since I came into the game. They would come out with us and drink wine when we had pints. We got one Spanish lad absolutely shit-faced on a team meal. He admitted that he very rarely drank, just had the occasional vodka and that's what he drank with us. We had a pint, he'd have a vodka.

We had to get him a cab home with a trusted taxi driver who looked after the players. The player was ill the next day and couldn't train, I don't think his body had ever experienced so much alcohol. The manager knew something was amiss and the captain came clean.

'Gaffer, it's our fault. We got him drinking.'

The manager fined him a week's wages and the players all covered it between them. The manager told the Spaniard not to associate with us. He just nodded. He couldn't speak English, but he got the message.

When I first started playing, the foreign players would do their time and then return to their home country. That happens less now. Their wives or girlfriends will often study or get a job – to keep the boredom away rather than for the money. The wife of one big name international told me that she dreamed of working in a Zara store in the nearby out of town shopping centre. That could have easily been sorted, especially in the months up to the Christmas rush like now.

But while the WAGs start their Christmas shopping in plenty of time, the players are thinking only about the games ahead, our increasingly tough schedule in the cold.

November

Mid-November and the English winter has arrived with the first frosts. The temperature barely struggles above zero by half nine in the morning when we walk out onto the training pitch. I played with a Mediterranean lad who'd never seen frost in his life until he came out to his car in the chilly early hours. He didn't know what to do and rang me.

'My car is covered in white. It's not snow. It's hard,' he said in a desperate voice. 'What do I do? I'm going to be late for training and the gaffer will go crazy.'

I thought about telling him to sprinkle Corn Flakes on his car to make the frost go away, but opted responsibly to tell him he needed to scrape it off.

'What is scrape?' came the reply.

Ah, the joys of learning a new language in a new country. I mentioned boiling some water in a kettle.

'What is a kettle?' Then I remembered, foreign players don't have kettles because they don't drink tea. So I settled for: 'Turn your heater on inside the car and wait. The white will go away.'

The same player had never seen his breath on a winter's day before. Watching him one morning in training was like watching a child on Christmas Day. Working with people from different countries is one of the best aspects of being a professional footballer. I'd never even heard of one region of Spain until I played alongside someone from there. Last year, we took a holiday there and it was as beautiful as we'd been told, the food and wine as good as he'd recommended. Memories of that summer seem very distant as the cold seeps into our bones.

The training pitches are becoming heavy, the goal areas worn. Grass stops growing in November, but pitch technology has improved immensely and even the training pitches are better than the Premier League pitches I once had to contend with.

The main change has been in drainage. Rain used to sit on the surface and create muddy pitches which slowed the game down. Sand was sprinkled on top to absorb water, but it wasn't the perfect solution. If too much sand was used in the construction of a pitch, it would drain too quickly, become too dry and crumble – that's when you'd see the dangerous sandpits after the winter, where some parts of the pitch were too hard and other bits too soft.

Now, plastic fibres are woven into the surfaces to strengthen them. Artificial lamps are used to help the grass grow in the winter – and even in the summer in the biggest stadiums where enough sunlight doesn't reach all parts of the pitch.

Pitches are important to players. Now I find it hard to

believe the poor standards of the playing surfaces at the start of my career. I once waited for a ball which bobbled so much over the divots and mounds that it didn't come to me and I looked an idiot who couldn't trap a bag of sand. And I dread to recall some of the pitches I played on as a kid. At one we had to remove glass from the goalmouth before we could play, while another was known as 'dog shit stadium' for obvious reasons. I'd like to say that it toughens you up and makes you a better footballer, forcing you to anticipate that the ball you receive or the pass you give might go astray, but it doesn't. I'm told that junior pitches have improved. Maybe I should get out of my bubble and go and see some soon.

At our club, we like to play attacking football and consequently we need pitches that are flat, with short grass so that the ball runs smoothly. Short grass means the ball has less resistance and can zip across the surface, whereas long grass – like they use for rugby – slows the ball down.

It's important that the groundsmen get it right. The players need to have confidence in the pitch and know that the ball will come to them on an even surface. Pitches are watered before the warm up so the tempo is quicker. Unless it's raining, when everything I've said doesn't matter.

You can control the pitches at home but not away; that's one area where clubs have home advantage, but in truth the pitches are far more uniform than they used to be. As a kid I played a reserve game at a lower league ground where the grass in the corners of the pitch was so long that your full boot was submerged in the vegetation. Their first team played the long ball into those corners, where strikers held it up and crossed for target men. Simple, ugly, effective.

NOVEMBER

While pitches have changed, the weather hasn't. The foreign lads have been wearing gloves since September, but now everyone is covering up with snoods, long johns and gloves. Replacements look like Egyptian mummies. Not every manager allows this – and that doesn't go down well with players. One gaffer told us: 'Wear what you want, but I need to see some skin, some knee.' That was his way of banning tights.

The cold brings out the best in some characters. Our assistant manager really steps to the fore as the temperature drops. He knows exactly how to deal with professionals who might not fancy it on a cold and frosty morning.

Firmly old school and not even an excellent coach, but the players like and respect him. He doesn't pretend to like the manager, but their relationship works in a good cop–bad cop way.

A top-level former player himself and most definitely a hard bastard, the assistant has seen it all. He started warming us up this morning and shouted: 'Hands up who likes the manager?' A couple of the younger lads or newer players raised their arms. The assistant who'd asked the question deliberately put his hands low and close to the floor, while sniggering to himself. Suddenly, the focus shifted from an anticipated bollocking after losing on Saturday to the assistant manager with his hands near his ankles. The manager didn't see this, but bounded over a few minutes later.

'X!' he shouted to his assistant. 'Are you thick? I told you to put the goals over there, not here.'

'What did I just ask you, boys?' asked the assistant. 'And some of you actually raised your hands to say you like him. You should feel ashamed.'

The manager twigged that he'd been talking about him.

'Have you been boring them all again, X?' shouted the manager. 'Which of your three stories from thirty years in football have you told them? The one about the only time a bird came onto you in a pre-season tour? Bet you didn't tell them that she looked like a tranny *and* that she knocked you back. Or was it the time when your pay packet was a pound short and you threatened to go on strike? Or was it your very own blockbuster, the one about the time you actually had a decent game, what was it, nine years into your career?'

The assistant shook his head, but laughed. As a player it is a joy to see them bouncing it off each other.

'He's changed since becoming a manager,' said the assistant, for our benefit but knowing that he was being heard. 'Used to be a nice fella. Respected throughout football. Soon as he got offered that manager's spot in the car park he wondered why the President of the United States wasn't ringing him up and inviting him around for a meal with his Mrs. The term 'big time' was invented for him. Used to go on holiday to Magaluf with the lads, now he goes to places in Italy that he can't even pronounce, yet complains that he can't get pie and chips when he's there.'

If there wasn't a player laughing before, then there was now.

'And I've agreed to work for him!' added the assistant. 'Why? Because he got me pissed, slipped something in my drink and because I felt sorry for him because he's got no mates. But I've given him my word and, as you know, I'm a man of honour. And because I'm a man of honour, I'm going to get you winning as many football matches as possible so that you can earn a few quid and bring your kids up not to be like your manager. Now let's get training.'

What a way to start the day, what a way to make us forget about the weather. We'd not giggled so much since someone spotted that the manager's wife wore leopard-print knickers at a function, the sly old fox.

Some assistants are as barmy as anything. I worked with one who had a specific party piece. He would climb onto the top of a wardrobe and then shit into a pint glass from four or five feet. He did it on international duty, he did it on domestic duty while working at a football club.

The same coach went to a prestigious awards dinner in London. As a speaker got up from his table, so did he.

'I'm really sorry, but I've got to leave early and won't be able to hear you speak,' he said, causing a distraction. 'I'll take my drink with me.'

With that, he poured his pint into his jacket pocket. His fellow diners were aghast. Players loved his juvenile humour.

We were warming up before a game in November when the away team had a Caribbean band. There's nothing like hearing a Caribbean band in Yorkshire in winter. The assistant gathered us around.

'I want you all ready,' he said. 'Ready to play. And you two,' he said, pointing to a couple of black players. 'You also need to be ready if any of the band members go down.'

Everyone laughed, including the black lads. Was that racist? It wasn't taken as such. The same assistant once called everyone around in training.

'Whites v blacks,' he said, before pointing to a mixed-race lad. 'And you can referee.' Everyone cracked up.

I'd played blacks v whites in training a few times. Most dressing rooms are roughly split 50/50 between black and white lads. The games were always played in good spirits and the black lads usually won.

A different coach from the same generation, in an attempt to liven up training, said: 'Right, practice match between the good-looking bastards and the ugly fuckers or those with distinguishing features.'

One player joined the good-looking team.

'What are you doing?' asked the coach. 'You have a distinguishing feature. You're black.'

The player, a full international, was livid.

'And are you going to manage us because you're a fat c**t?' he queried. He ripped his bib off and told the manager that he was a racist. They didn't speak for months. The coach was a dinosaur from a bygone era and got exactly what he deserved. I never heard him make such a comment again. Even he realised he had to change.

I've outlined some incidents which are toe-curlingly racist, but racism is not the issue people think it is in football, because racist incidents are very rare. They shouldn't happen at all, but it frustrates me when I read the always negative headlines about racism in the game. What about the positives, the success of multi-culturalism in football, where an African can play next to an Argentinian, a white boy from Bradford can become best friends with a black Mancunian and play for club and country together?

I've played with black lads all through my career. I doubt I would have come across so many people with a different skin colour had I stayed in my home town. There's no way I would have become close mates with black lads from estates where white people are treated with suspicion and they would never have been part of my world, where black faces are rarely seen.

Being a footballer has made me a better person, more cosmopolitan and tolerant. Skin colour ceased to be an issue from the minute I became an apprentice and walked into a dressing room with numerous black players. Bullying, financial matters and players being groomed by outside influences like agents are all bigger flashpoints in a dressing room.

When players are asked about race in football, which they often are, they have to say the right thing, while half the time wondering what the fuss is about.

It's the same when the Let's Kick Racism out of Football road show comes to the training ground once a season. We wear the T-shirt and smile for the photos, while all the time feeling bemused.

I've been in football all my life and can count on my fingers the number of racist incidents I've witnessed. And is banter racism? The black lads at one club, especially those of a mixed race, used to pull far better women than the white boys. They'd hammer us for it, asking us if we needed any help.

'You going to learn how to get a woman by watching the brothers tonight?' one player asked me. It was light-hearted banter. It was also true.

'If your Mrs wants a bit of black, let me know, bro,' was another line that I had no answer to.

Players know that racism was a bigger problem in football from the 1970s and 80s, when black players started to break into sides in significant numbers. Then, I'm told that one manager used to say to any unhappy black player 'Wogs wrong with you?' On another occasion, a manager instructed his players to pick the cones up after training. One player lifted one of the black lads off his feet.

'What are you doing?' asked the manager.

'I thought you said pick the coons up,' replied the player. The black player actually laughed at it in a dressing room where anything went.

There was evident racism on the terraces, chants like: 'Trigger, trigger, trigger, shoot that nigger.' I love the story about Paul Parker, when the entire Stretford End sang that at him while he played for QPR.

Parker made a 'gun' with his fingers, pointed it at his head, looked up at the sea of 10,000 faces and pretended to shoot himself in the head. Those racist bigots who thought they would humiliate and intimidate him were silenced. Parker had confronted and outwitted them. Two years later, he was playing in front of those very fans as a Manchester United player. Such chants would be unimaginable now.

I've never heard racism from the terraces in England, but I have while playing international football in Poland and Italy. In both cases, monkey noises were made when black players touched the ball. The players were not outwardly upset. They pitied those backward, racist idiots, saw it as a sign of weakness and lack of education.

'You must be gutted how your life has worked out,' I said to one of the lads. 'International footballer. Beautiful family. Financial stability. Idolised by thousands. Bet you'd swap it all to pay and stand with a load of racists and pretend to be a monkey.' He laughed. Had the racism come from his own fans it might have been different, but he was able, at least on the surface, to shrug it off.

Not every assistant manager is a touch crazy with a line in sub-racist banter. Other first-team coaches are wet lettuces, or BBCs as we call them – balls, bibs, cones. They will be the manager's mate, looked after with a nice job after doing all their coaching badges. They've probably known the manager for twenty years and the manager feels that he can trust them.

There's another, completely different type of assistant – the hard bastard. He can be the foil to the softly spoken manager, the one to back him up with his presence on the bench if there is any trouble between the benches. They can be effective partnerships.

The hard assistant (or sometimes the big goalkeeper coach) often provides the muscle too. Look around at the assistant managers, there are some real hard bastards about. I worked with one who suffered no fools. He called fans 'civilians' and thought they knew nothing. He stood by his boss (and still does) in the Premier League, backing him up when there were any touchline disputes. He once called one of the best-known managers a 'prick' and a 'charlatan' to his face.

He also halted training when a player chipped the goalkeeper on the grounds that 'you won't have the balls to do that in a match, so don't do it now' and stopped a fight in a tunnel after a game by windmilling between the rival players, pushing them all into their respective dressing rooms. He then shouted to our opponents: 'Take a breather and have a think if you want to fight me one-on-one.' They didn't. Just as his own players were agreeing, he turned on us and said: 'The same goes for you lot. There's not a fight in any of you.'

The one-man vigilante had just done what four police officers and six stewards had failed to achieve. To him, it was all part of being a good assistant.

It's really important that the players get on with the assistant. They have to trust him. They know that he's going to tell the manager things, but he can't tell them everything.

I was having a few marital problems and the assistant had a word, offering support and explaining that he'd gone through a divorce. I was quite open with him, but I sensed he had gone straight to the manager to pass the information on which I considered a breach of confidence. My problems were not serious enough to affect my game and they were sorted out, but I didn't appreciate it when the manager asked for a word and asked if I'd like a week or two off, even if he was trying to help.

Another breach – more amusing but still a breach – came when I was spotted in McDonald's. My wife was visiting family, so I took my son for a Happy Meal and sat eating in the front window. I played well the following day and started returning to the same place to eat the same food before games. It was a risk as we weren't supposed to eat fast food. Being recognised every two minutes wasn't ideal either, but the superstition lodged in my head.

On one visit, I saw the assistant manager's car out of the corner of my eye. It was definitely him, because the manager called me into his office after training the next day and fined me for eating junk. I marked the assistant's card as a grass who couldn't be trusted and put the word out amongst the lads.

I like the assistant to be a character, one of several in the dressing room because that's what I've grown up with. Characters are what make being a footballer enjoyable, the people who provide the everyday laughs, even if it's at your expense.

When I broke into the first team, we stayed in London after one game and set up a big night out. I was told to come along and that money wouldn't be needed. It was my first night out with the team and I wasted £120 on a Valentino shirt for the occasion. I told myself that I was ready to hang around with the main men and was really up for the night out when we headed to one of the best bars in the West End. Someone had sorted it for us on the door so there were no problems getting in. A group of fifteen of us got everyone's attention as we strolled in, perhaps because some of us were easily recognisable faces, or because fifteen lads walking into any bar would stand out. I saw girls looking at me who would never have looked at me before, smelling professional foot-ballers – and everything that came with them.

The team captain walked over to me. We hadn't spoken much, he had a cruel-to-be-kind policy with younger players.

'You've been doing well,' he said. 'You're one of the lads now. Can I get you a drink?'

The words lifted me so much. Here was the top boy in the dressing room complimenting me.

'Yes, please,' I replied nervously, sounding like the new kid on his first day at secondary school.

'Tell you what,' said the captain, 'it's my round, I'll get them in. Order three bottles of champagne for the boys, I'll nip to the toilet and I'll be back in a minute and we'll have a chat.'

I felt honoured that the skipper trusted me to order three bottles of Veuve Cliquot. I was anxious and excited as the bottles arrived.

'That's £187, please,' said the barman.

'No problem, I'm waiting for my mate,' I replied. And I waited. And waited. And I realised that I was alone, because the whole team had gone. I called three different teammates on my mobile, the younger guys who I knew best, and the phone rang out with each. I was left standing like a lemon – and with no money on me because the lads told me that everything would be taken care of.

'Is there a problem?' asked the girl behind the bar.

I explained the situation and she called her manager over.

'So, you've ordered three bottles of champagne and we've opened them all – and now you're telling me that you can't pay for them?' he said.

I was flustered and didn't have a clue what to do. The manager knew that the lads had spent a lot of money in there and that we weren't complete blaggers. I left my watch at the bar and went to find them in a bar down the road. They were all laughing at me as I walked in. The captain went back to the bar and sorted it out. They told the manager and he laughed at me too. My name was Champagne Charlie for at least a month. Once bitten . . .

I learned very quickly that anything goes in the dressing room, whether it's jokes about race, cancer or family. One footballer who didn't play for us, but who was close to us socially fell very ill. He came to see us after training as he lived locally. We wanted to make a fuss of him because he was genuinely popular. So he joined us in the dressing room after one session and the lads were pleased to see him. The captain shouted for silence, then stood up and said: 'We need to have a night out with X because he won't be here in three months.' The poorly player stood there shaking his head. He was laughing, but he couldn't believe what he was hearing. 'And we need a whip round for his coffin, lads. Needs to be a decent one with gold-plated handles.'

Thankfully he later recovered from his illness.

That poorly player was a decent person and I can't say that of all in my profession. We have a little issue here with one of our best players. The best one, actually. And the issue is that he's a bit of a knob. He doesn't train as hard as he should, he frequently turns up late and last week asked if he could make his own way to an away game as it was closer to his house than where the team were meeting.

Any other manager would have fired him off, but there's one mitigating circumstance: he's brilliant and more than covers for his foibles when he plays. Or, as the manager explained in private to a couple of senior players: 'I know he's a nightmare, but he wins football games for me on a Saturday.'

He annoys those other players, but he wins games for them too, bringing in more nice, fat win bonuses. We've chosen to tolerate him and balance the fact that he's an egg against the fact that he is a proven match-winner.

When a manager isn't good at man-management, a difficult but brilliant player can be his biggest problem. At one club, the cocky but talented best player turned up late for training. The manager, who struggled to handle him, felt under pressure to act and bellowed across the training pitch: 'That's a fine for being late.'

The player, a real fan favourite who was becoming a big fish is a small pond, looked at his boss with contempt and replied, 'Bothered.'

'Two weeks,' added the manager.

'I bet you don't fine me,' replied the player. 'And if you do, I hope you've got change from a million pound note.' The other players laughed and the manager's humiliation was complete.

The player had all the power. He knew other clubs wanted him and that his current club were going to cash in on him at some point. So he acted like a complete knob and, just as he predicted, he still didn't get fined.

Not only individuals behave badly. I was at one club where a clique of three players routinely pushed the boundaries. Their arrogance came from a combination of factors: they were among the best players, they were close to the chairman and the manager was too soft.

During a game, one of the three was substituted and shook his head in anger as he walked off slowly. The manager should have bollocked him, but he didn't. Instead, he pretended to make light of the situation in training the following Monday by re-enacting the moody player walking off. He went to great efforts to do this like wearing the player's shirt and getting his physio to play manager. It fell flat. The other players were baffled and the moody sub actually said: 'I'm embarrassed for you, bruv.'

At another club, a player arrived with a big transfer fee and reputation. He was very good, but the manager had the shock of his life in the dressing room before his first game.

'I don't play on the left wing anymore,' explained the left winger who'd been bought, not entirely unsurprisingly, to play as a left winger, 'I play a more central role now.' The manager told him to play on the left but the player continued and said: 'I don't think you understand. I don't play on the left anymore.'

Not wanting to upset his new signing, the manager relented and played him in the middle, with the usual central midfielder consigned to the wing. It unbalanced the whole team and the manager had to explain to his opinionated chairman that the new left winger he'd paid seven figures for wasn't a left winger any more.

'Are you taking the piss out of me?' replied the chairman.

Players can only usually get away with terrible behaviour if they are the best at the club, but they don't stand a chance if they are not. I saw one foreign lad arrive at our club with a good reputation after being recommended by a legendary manager.

He was put into the reserves for his first game to judge his match fitness. What he did was catch the ball during play, walk over to the referee and explain that it was too hard and hurting his head when he headed it. It probably was too hard, and the ref was prepared to humour him, going to the bench with his eyebrows raised and swapping balls.

In the second half, the player took a knock on his leg and held the game up as he asked for the physio to rub Deep Heat. In-between his toes. When he turned out to be a let-down as a player and completely unsuited to the English game, he was left with no chance. His career in England ended almost before it started and yet had he been any good, the rest of the players would have probably started rubbing Deep Heat between their toes.

We've got a couple of big away games coming up. It amuses me when people say that a team will be fearful of going to a certain away ground because of the hostile atmosphere. I've played at all the big English grounds and not felt intimidated at one.

Maybe it was different before the Taylor Report in 1990 and all-seater stadiums, but the mouthy fans don't tend to be as loud when they are sitting down and easily identifiable, rather than sounding off behind someone on a packed terrace.

The media exaggerate the importance of the atmosphere. I've not played in Istanbul where it's famously hostile, but I've played with players who have. Even they say that once the game is underway, it becomes background noise. The atmosphere has almost no bearing on the result of the game. It becomes the norm and you'd be worried if there was no noise.

I've been at away grounds where I've been singled out for abuse. Doesn't bother me one bit. In fact it's an acknow-ledgement that I can play. Rival fans pick on good players and I know some who actually feed off the abuse. Like I said earlier, it's when your own fans start to boo that you have real problems.

I got a lift back from one away game and bumped into a group of the fans at the services, fans I knew had been giving me dog's abuse at games. Not one of them said a word to me. Cowards. I was right for punching them, but I couldn't. My mate was even keener about punching them, but I persuaded him that it wasn't a good idea to wade into a group of spotty eighteen-year-olds.

I eventually won those fans over and the club subsequently made a large profit on me, but I never forgot those ultra-critical fans who got on my back when I started out.

The worst ground to play at in England is Millwall. That's where you get called a paedophile for no reason, but it still doesn't affect your performance. Sticks and stones and all that. We did a warm down after one game at the New Den and I witnessed a woman come out from a hospitality area and encourage the Millwall manager to 'lay the cunts out'. As in us, the away team.

The hours spent on a coach on a motorway can be a grind, but an away day is no different to a school trip. You've got twenty-five lads on a jolly to do something they like. Some players have mistresses in other towns, some managers have them too. It's all done very discreetly, but as with a school outing, the managers have to appear to be keeping control of their little charges.

There's another big game for me this month against my former club. Don't let anyone tell you otherwise: every player wants to get one over his former club. And when he does, like scoring a winning goal at the ground where he once played, it's the best feeling in the world. He might not celebrate the goal like normal, but the feeling inside is as good as winning a trophy. I know; I've been there.

I spent the week before going back to the club who sold me (for a lot of money) doing media interviews. I didn't want to, but I was told that all the media requests were for me. I can understand why, journalists need to hook their story onto something.

I talked a load of clichéd nonsense about wanting my former club to do well – apart from on Saturday. The journalists would laugh at that one like it was actually funny. It was the first lie in what was an insincere game of charades. I complimented former teammates I despised and praised fans who'd made me a hero one week and a villain the next, the cyber cowards who slaughtered me hiding behind their stupid little forum names if I didn't turn it on like Messi every week. The fans who said it was good business when I was sold. And, most satisfying, the fans who stood silent as I wheeled away from the goal after getting the winner. I didn't overdo the celebration, class dictates that, but it was the most beautiful buzz, the cleanest hit of adrenaline I've ever felt.

I held it all in until I got back on the team coach. Then I punched the air and let out my emotions. As our coach pulled away from the ground, I put two fingers up to the home fans – while hiding behind a curtain. Childish, I know, but it felt fantastic and my new teammates enjoyed it.

Going back is weird. And not all negative. I was genuinely pleased to see all the members of staff that I'd got on well with. They whispered to me that I should never have been sold. And some former teammates, but why would I want a former club to do better without me? That would surely reflect badly on me as a footballer.

I've yet to meet a pro who doesn't feel the same. I moved to a club and found myself next to a big name in the dressing room, big for his exploits at his former club rather than the one we played for together. He was a hero at his old club. Still is. While I was there, my old team beat his old team. His reaction surprised me. I thought that he would have wanted his old side to win. He didn't. He told me that he'd slid across his lounge floor when the goal went in and asked me to ring the goalscorer and tell him that he was going to send him a bottle of champagne. Players seldom leave football clubs on their own terms and it grates, sometimes for years, because they thought they could do better, stay another year or earn a bigger contract.

I know another who went back to his former club, Nottingham Forest. He was a bit of a tearaway and he drew a moustache on a framed picture of Brian Clough in the club reception. The Forest suit welcoming people to the club was quite rightly fuming.

There's another thing when you play away. Hotels, with time to kill. The bat phones will come out and the aim will be for players to get girls to send them suggestive photos, the more flesh showing and the more explicit the pose the better. These will, naturally, be passed about without the female's knowledge.

They might not have even met the girls in person, but through social media. Players get loads of texts and tweets, but they tend to pay attention only if they come from beautiful girls. Some of the girls know exactly what they are doing. They will start out with an innocent compliment such as: 'Good game at the weekend.' The standard cagey response is: 'Thanks,' and it is up to the female to progress matters to online flirting. Once he knows that he has a live one, the player will just try his luck. He'll quickly shift the conversation to private via messages on Facebook or Direct messages on Twitter. Then the girl, or he, might get a bit cheeky.

My roommate met a nice girl in an airport lounge. She was a dancer returning back to her city from Europe. He fancied her too, but he's the faithful kind, one of the few. She swapped emails and within a week she'd sent him a picture of herself asking for his opinion on what to wear on her night out with friends later on. The first asked if he could see her knicker line through the dress she was wearing and, if so, she would wear no knickers. The second, in a different dress, asked if she was better wearing a bra or not. And the third simply asked 'or would this be better?' and was a picture of her in saucy underwear. He offered his opinion and left it at that. Ninety per cent of footballers wouldn't.

Other girls might be old flings or fully-fledged mistresses. They might even come along to the hotel and a player might sneak them into a room.

What do the girls get out of it? Sex. Sex with an often good-looking rich and famous young man in his physical prime. They also might hope that it might lead to something more substantial, even if it seldom does.

The headline story about the players 'roasting' a girl in a London hotel a decade ago didn't surprise me. A dangerous game, but one some footballers and girls are willing to risk. There's another phrase used, 'play me in'. It's a term from the pitch. Off the pitch, it means this: someone gets a girl back to the hotel and, when they are finished, 'play me in' so that I can have sex with her too. There are many willing female participants in this. But it can go horribly wrong if a girl isn't up for it. Like when the player texted his teammate while he was having sex, encouraging him to come and join them. He said he had cleared it and it was OK with the girl. It wasn't. The player then arrived in the room, but the girl didn't appreciate it all and started crying. She calmed down, but there was always the danger that she may have gone to the authorities.

The players have to be wary of blackmail and demands for money. An old teammate paid a girl £5,000 to keep her quiet and stop her going to the papers. His wife was a gorgeous model and the story would have been too juicy to resist.

Not paying up could lead to kiss-and-tell tabloid stories. I've known single players who aren't particularly bothered by the kiss-and-tell stories, so long as the girls speak well of their performance. And I've known married players worm their way out of a tabloid exposé by describing it publicly as 'nonsense' or 'ludicrous' (and therefore not actually denying it) and claiming that: 'She's made it up to make money out of us.' That can be enough for a partner as that's what she wants to hear. Maybe, deep down, she suspects that her man isn't always faithful. Others are naïve, others plain thick. The wife of one teammate, asked if she had the right visa ahead of a holiday to America, pulled out her Visa credit card.

Some players, as I've said, justify their behaviour on the grounds that 'We don't drink, do drugs or smoke, allow us one vice.' One manager welcoming a new signing with a reputation for enjoying himself, refused to condemn it, instead saying: 'I've heard you like beers and birds, son. You score plenty of goals for me and I'll get you both.'

The higher you go, the more sophisticated the arrangements become. In Madrid and Milan, fixers make sure there are groups of 'safe' girls – that is, groups of stunning females who will be discreet and not talk. Not prostitutes, but girls who like to sleep with footballers in return for access to the best parties.

When I started playing, I never heard of players using prostitutes. They didn't need to. That has changed and it's not about those players' inability to attract other women – that is never a problem for a professional footballer, whatever you look like, you have to fight them off. Prostitutes are seen as a safe bet because they won't talk. Well, that's the theory. Some players have been exposed by prostitutes, but the chances of being 'blown up' – shopped – by a prostitute are slimmer.

There are other problems with this. Women start to get treated as objects, judged on how they look. Players don't talk about what a great woman she is, how they respect her as a person. They talk about her tits and arse.

One or two former colleagues have been obsessed with sleeping with as many different girls as possible, getting their buzz from the (usually successful) thrill of the chase. A normal relationship becomes impossible because they know they can get near instant highs on tap. They became addicted to sex.

There can be a heavy price to pay. The mood after one away win changed after our manager gathered us around and said: 'Someone in this room has been a silly boy. And that someone was me.' He went on to explain that he'd had a fling and that the papers had the story, which they'd print the following day. He said he'd done it once and wouldn't do it again and that we should ignore it and move on. He then went home and told his wife the same thing. From what we understand, it was far more difficult for his wife to move on than it was for the players and all in the month before Christmas too.

As December approaches, my 'replacement', who looked majestic in August, doesn't look the same player. It's a cliché because it's true.

The foreign lads have brought many benefits. Talent, for one. And they're more professional when it comes to looking after themselves. I've never been a big drinker, but I almost stopped completely when I saw how well one of the Spanish players looked after himself.

He was into protein and vitamin shakes before they became the norm. You have to replace fluids after exercise. It used to be water, now every player has their own shake bottle at the training ground made up to how they like it. Players become very attached to their bottles, they become part of their routine and they get upset when they go missing, get angry when someone fills them with Coca-Cola.

The change was gradual. I can recall one old school manager asking if the protein drink I had helped me win a 50/50 tackle away at West Brom. Of course not, but if you look after yourself, eat well and drink well then you are far more likely to get in the team where you can have a chance of winning that tackle. If you don't, there's no place for you in the modern game.

Having said all that, Paul Scholes is one of the best, if not the best, English players of recent times. He's asthmatic and not an athlete. I'm not saying that he has pie and chips every day. He is blessed with god-given skill, though, and no amount of magic powder in a bottle can give me what he has.

December

December is party season for most people and footballers are no different. Every one of us looks forward to the players' Christmas party, the one we organise for ourselves – and which have become notorious over the years – but there are plenty of other functions to negotiate. Being high profile, we receive piles of invites to various places and while we can't attend them all, some are compulsory.

Everyone has to show their face at the party for club employees. At one former club, I spotted a coach kissing a secretary in a shop doorway outside where the party was being held. He put his finger across his lips and a teammate and I swore we'd say nothing. Which was a complete and utter lie as, naturally, we told everyone at the first opportunity.

Two days later in training, we persuaded the canteen chef to put two seats aside for the coach and the secretary. Warming to the task, he popped out and bought candles and some heart-shaped glitter, plus a posh tablecloth and some name tags for the pair. The married coach was mortified when he came in from training, but took it on the chin.

The staff party at our club is a particular favourite of the chairman who wants us to feel like we're one big happy family and are all the same, when in fact some of the staff are on the minimum wage, others are interns on nothing and others earn millions of pounds. Per year, before tax.

But for one evening, at least, we mingle freely – so the young pro can make a move on the girl he fancies from the ticket office – or can try – and the club chaplain makes a beeline for the match programme editor and attempts to engage her in a conversation about higher matters than football.

The party is the chairman's idea. Some chairmen keep their distance, you only ever see them at the training ground when things aren't going well. Our current one is more hands on. He calls every member of staff including the players by their first name. That's a lot to remember, but he prides himself on it. He also asks that we call him by his first name. He's a good people person and you can see why he's done well in life.

The staff party is held at a function room at the stadium, with a meal thrown in – but drinks have to be paid for. We players stay for a couple of hours before dropping our shoulder and heading off with an excuse about not wanting to stay out late because we've got big games coming up. We have three or four beers, nothing heavy.

It's good to mix with staff. I see some of them every day and have a great deal of time for them. One of the kit ladies who help out the kitman has a husband who works in a garage and I go to him if I need new tyres.

The chairman stands up and says a few words on the microphone about the season so far. He's positive as ever and hopes that we can push on for a European place. The word 'Europe' excites everyone, but it's going to be hard for us to finish in the top six. We're middle of the road in every way. Still, every team needs a target. 'Let's aim for mid-table' doesn't quite do it.

The chairman has also been known to hold barbecues at his farm for all the staff, though there hasn't been one for two years since two players blotted their copybooks. I wasn't there, but they decided that they would have a race on two donkeys grazing quietly in the adjacent field. One fell off and hurt his shoulders. The manager, who felt that he had to show who was the boss, was fuming. The chairman too. I can't imagine the donkeys were that thrilled either.

The players' party is a completely different matter. The captain sorts everything, with lobbying from the other players who will tell him where we want to go. He'll ask around for dates and locations and come to a decision. This year's venue is Manchester after an away game at one of the city's clubs.

All twenty-five professionals at the club are invited. A very senior player might get away with bringing a mate along if that mate was known to others or if he was a player himself, but the general ground rule is 'players and that's it'. The more people there not from the group, the more risk of any misdemeanours getting out. The cast-iron rule is that what happens on the Christmas party stays on the Christmas party, yet even if only the players are present, they talk – to their mates, their agent, their partners. Keeping anything secret at a football club is hard and even an innocent answer to a question when you are out and about can become insider information. Tell the concerned supermarket cashier why you are limping and might not be fit for Saturday, and the internet will do the rest.

That's why there's a rule that no photos are to be taken. Manchester United went as far as banning phones. Some of us will be recognised in a Manchester bar, a lot of us won't.

There are very good reasons why players want Christmas party shenanigans to be kept secret. I've seen hired strippers going backstage to perform extra duties and nobody batting an eyelid, this during a time when a footballer can't afford to lose focus over the festive period – apart from the odd prank or four to mark the season of goodwill.

There was one club with two very high-profile players who didn't like each other. They were opposites. The team was doing Secret Santa like in so many offices up and down the land. Each of them drew a name of someone they had to buy a present for. A defender who was struggling for form received a book telling him how to play soccer which was gleefully presented to him in front of the other players.

A lad with notoriously bad breath opened his to find a packet of dog biscuits, which he wasn't particularly happy about, but the draw was especially unkind to the two members of the dressing room who really hated each other. Naturally, at the other club, the enemies drew each other and had to present their carefully chosen gifts in front of an expectant dressing room.

One of the pair bought the other a dildo and hung a mini kit with the player's name on the back.

'Here you go,' he said. 'That's because you are the biggest prick in the team.'

The lad was fuming and it split the team because it wasn't a joke. Some saw the funny side; others thought he'd gone too far. Later that night, the insulted player got his revenge. He smothered his mouth and nose with chocolate cake and shouted: 'Right everybody, who am I? Here's a clue, I've just left the manager's office.' The other player henceforth hated him even more. They barely spoke a word to each other after that.

Other pranks have gone way too far. One manager was a famous disciplinarian and was respected by the players, but he was absent for one away trip in December as he had to attend a funeral. Managers attend a lot of funerals, either because they have to represent the club or because they feel bad not attending when invited. The well-known also tend to know a lot of people.

In his absence, the lads went on the beer and ignored the curfew set by the assistant manager. The captain – a top-level international – left his phone on the bar and one of the strikers decided to ring the manager, late in the evening.

The striker was a character and did an unconvincing impersonation of the captain. He told him that the lads were going to have a few more beers but that he would encourage them as it was important for team bonding. The manager was livid. He suspected who'd made the call and absolutely bollocked, then fined, the impressionist. We blamed the captain for leaving his phone unguarded – a big no-no.

DECEMBER

We opened up one player's phone to find a video of him making love to his wife. That was quickly blue-toothed around the whole squad. The player was devastated and so upset that he told the manager who made sure that everyone deleted it off their phones.

Another young teammate fell for a local girl who was at the staff Christmas party, even though she didn't work for the club. The lad was a thick Mancunian – he once thought that a chateaubriand steak was a fine red wine – but he was the club's rising star. He was very loud on the subject of the charms of his new love. Three months into the relationship, the captain started grilling him in front of everyone in the dressing room.

'Do you love your new bird?' he asked.

'Yes,' replied the player, sheepishly.

'Could she be the one for you?'

'Yeah.'

'So how do you feel that he's shagged her and so has he and so has he?' he said, pointing to several players who had indeed enjoyed the lad's girlfriend. He was crushed and cried in front of all of us. You learn quickly not to brag in a changing room.

The venue of the Christmas party depends on what level you play at. They used to be held in a bar in the city where your club was situated. Sometimes they still are, but there's a big disadvantage for the player here because their partner will expect them home. And there's another: they don't want to be recognised talking to another girl by the wife's hairdresser, or collared by a drunken bore who wants to discuss tactics. We deserve a night out as a team once in a while where we can act a bit silly.

That's why there has been a recent trend for jumping out of the goldfish bowl and going to Dublin, London or wherever a good time can be had without too much recognition – with the exception of beautiful, available girls, as a famous face makes the chase all the easier.

Some players would be recognised wherever they went. Manchester United players would be identified whether they went out in Manchester or Malaysia. So they stay in Manchester, where they've hired entire hotels and the best-looking girls in the city are invited by scouts through model agencies or the perfume and cosmetic counters at the pricier department stores. Every girl in that city would spend months trying to get on the guest list for the United party.

All of this appalls the managers, but the problem is that they were once players themselves. It's like the parent telling his kids what not to do . . . but remembering what they did.

Our current manager has a saying which I like. 'Remember who you are, what you are and where you are,' he counsels. The manager will tell you to behave and that you'd better be good in training on the Thursday. Most footballers get Wednesday off, so a party would be on a Tuesday night. There are clubs in London which are full of footballers on a Tuesday night throughout the year, but they get busiest before Christmas. Places like Funky Buddha in Mayfair, where you have to be on the guest list to get in. Unless you are a beautiful woman.

Take a Christmas party in London. Our manager's wise words are soon forgotten on one Christmas do as we pile into a bar in Covent Garden early in the afternoon and straight on the beer. We don't get to drink over Christmas, so we like to make the players' parties as memorable as possible. After more beers in more bars, we have a meal, followed by a strip club and then a proper club. Party organisers would make sure that there were handpicked girls at the club.

But for this year, we've looked north. The team coach will return without us after the game because we've booked a five-star hotel in the city and fixed access for a couple of the best places. How? Doesn't every dressing room in England have a Mancunian, a Scouser, a Geordie and a Londoner? Or someone who has played in those places and has a phone full of contacts to help us out.

We manage a hard-fought draw in Manchester. The unexpectedly good result has us all buzzing and we go back to the hotel pumped. Play well and that feeling can last until the next match, a week-long high. We get changed in the hotel and meet in the bar downstairs, a smart place already heaving with guests, wealthy people who've been at the game and the local socialites. A few people recognise us, but not so much that it's a pain. A few lads order a sandwich or something light from the bar, until the centre half pipes up that 'eating's cheating'.

A fleet of taxis drives us to the bar where they know we're coming. The Mancunian teammate has reserved us two tables (with a minimum spend of £3,000 each). A stunning girl on the door holding a clipboard welcomes us in like royalty, asking us if they need to take our jackets. The security guys stand impassively. The others in the queue, including girls in barely-there tops, towering heels and skin-tight skirts, either goggle at us or try and work out who we are.

There are some football teams that are seen as a liability

even by those places anxious to take their money, but when you're a Premier League footballer doors open for you. Bars and hotels salivate at the potential profits, both from players who will spend money like water and the other guests who will be trying to spend players' money for them.

We have two large tables in a booth. Most of the lads stand up around them rather than sit down. Champagne chills in ice buckets and, beyond a small red rope, very hot girls, all lookers, try to act nonchalant showing off their boob tubes, big hair, orange spray tans and fake Christian Louboutin shoes. Or maybe the Louboutins are genuine, but I speak to a few of them and they're council estate girls. There's nothing wrong with a council estate, but these girls will need someone to subsidise their pleasures. The £15 or so in their purses will just about get them a couple of drinks. And we're happy to oblige them tonight. Or, rather, the even prettier group just beyond them.

We send a young pro on a scouting mission around the bar. He comes back and confirms that the group we'd spotted are the best-looking. They've spotted us too, how could they miss twenty-odd fit, expensively dressed young men? He's sent back and asks a group of three or four of the girls if they'd like to share a glass of champagne. Of course they would. Soon, our table has as many girls around it as men. There are two ice buckets of champagne in the middle and a gorgeous waitress who brings more bottles and glasses to replace the ones smeared with lipstick. I speak to one girl who asks where I'm from. She thinks it's part of Manchester. It's not.

Another player tells another girl that he's from Reykjavik.

He's not, but he gives the same story to everyone. She tells him that her friend was a holiday rep there last summer. I think she mixed up the capital of Iceland with a Greek island.

One or two of the Man United and City lads join us too. Teams can be huge rivals among fans, but the players can get on well.

I'm up for it. I've played well, the team has played well, we've got a result and we're having a great night. The music is good, the drink is flowing, the place is packed and bubbling on a Saturday night. Mind, it would be the same if we'd played poorly, but we didn't and our cake has a nice big cherry on it.

We have a fantastic time, all the better in my eyes for being without the seedy debauchery of past Christmas functions. You can't really start a food fight in a smart bar without getting ejected, but you can still act the big man by spraying champagne about. Nobody does that, though – unaccountably we're all showing a bit of class. Nearly. I spot a condom draped over a girl's shoulder. She's no idea that it's there as she pouts and flirts. The players, especially the one who went to the toilet, bought it, opened it up and put it on her shoulder, find it hilarious. A friend points it out to her and she's none too happy.

The group starts to fragment at one. Some of the lads go to a casino and stay until 6 a.m. Others pull girls and take them back to the hotel. One pulls a girl who refuses to go back to the hotel with him because she doesn't want to seem easy. She's staying at a friend's, so my steamingly drunk teammate offers to take her home in a taxi.

'I live in Barrow,' she says.

'That's fine,' he replies.

'It's over an hour away.'

'That's fine,' says the player, 'just as long as I can take you home safely.'

She agrees to this. He went back to Barrow and slept with the girl, then he got a taxi back to Manchester in the morning, £500 worse off after two taxis and three hours driving. He could have squandered much more in the casino. All in all, it was a successful weekend in Manchester and we've behaved ourselves, more or less. But that hasn't always been the case, by a long way.

There was one Christmas do when five strippers were hired to perform during the meal. They started to strip between the players, who were split into two groups sitting around on chairs in a bar. I knew it was just a question of time before something happened, and it soon did.

'Have you wiped your arse, love?' shouted the centre forward at one of the girls, who was manoeuvring around us in a thong. She forced a smile.

The girls had been instructed which players they were to embarrass – namely the young boys. Humiliation rather than sex is the chief aim of the process. The strippers selected their young targets by pointing at them. One was absolutely mortified, the other a very willing participant as he was stripped down to his boxer shorts. A tie taken off another player was wrapped around the neck of the younger 'victim'. He was then led around like a dog on a lead. The stripper pulled his boxer shorts down and sprayed whipped cream up his backside. Then walked away from him.

The other player was made to lie on the floor in his boxers while a stripper straddled him and simulated sex. The lad became notably excited, even though he didn't want to be. As did the rest of us, even the bloke drinking beer from a pint glass with a stripper's thong in it.

Then she tore his boxers so that he couldn't wear them again, before putting cream around his balls and licking it off until he became even more aroused. She then got up, walked off and left him lying naked on the floor, obviously utterly humiliated, to loud cheering.

The girls regrouped to do a final strip, which couldn't be completed because a player threw a sausage roll across the strippers into the other group. A food fight inevitably ensued, with the dessert table providing ample ammunition until one of the strippers was hit in the face by a chocolate cake and their minder took them off the stage and away. We had our own minders, two local security guys. Our 'people' smoothed things with their 'people'. How very Hollywood.

We'd had a laugh and forgot about it, but the club got a call a few days later telling the manager that the strippers were going to sell their story to a tabloid for the princely sum of two grand.

A senior player was dispatched to sort out the mess. He offered them £2,500. The girls settled on £3,000. Well within our means and the club's name was bigger than most of the players', but it was an expensive food fight all the same as the players had to chip in.

I'd watched the faces around me when the cake was flying, not that interested in joining in myself. Some had got completely carried away and were at the heart of it, others thought it amusing, while you could see others thinking 'What an earth am I doing here?'

But no one went home and we crawled as a pack to the next bar, where the potential for trouble trebled as it was open to the public. Word quickly spread and the bar was busier than normal for 6 p.m. on a Wednesday night in early December. A fan came over and asked me about a forthcoming game. He was alright, a lad of a similar age to me. I had a chat with him until I heard: 'Why don't you fuck off and leave us alone?' from another, very drunk player, directed at the fan. The fan would have been within his rights to kick off, instead he went to leave, but not before I'd apologised on behalf of my plastered teammate. There was no need for what he did, but at least the drunk chose a target outside the team for his anger. Tension between players is never far away on Christmas night outs.

Eventually the night began to fragment and our group started to split into threes and fours heading either home to the hotel for bed, to a lap dancing club or a casino. It was barely 9 p.m. and most were in a pitiful state.

There's a legendary story among players about one team's Christmas party, where they had arranged to meet up in fancy dress. One of the reserve lads hired a pantomime horse outfit and wore a United shirt with 'van Nistelrooy' on the back. The lad, who was on £800 a week – about 1% of what Ruud took home – was lucky to be in his company, but that didn't bother him. The only thing was, he got stuck in traffic and arrived an hour late, just after the players had sat down to eat a meal. They looked up to see a horse walk in. The senior players were in stitches, the Dutch striker was not.

* * *

DECEMBER

The changing room is much more than a place where you change clothes – there's always some kind of deal or scheme on offer. One lad at a former club had a contact who could get high-end designer toiletries. He was selling presentation boxes which would usually be £150 for roughly half that, so most of us put the orders in.

Footballers are paranoid about being ripped off, about workmen, who know they have got money, quoting them too much for a job at their house, so they like a bargain.

A teammate bought one of the boxes for his mum for Christmas, but while he was out training I meticulously unwrapped the packaging and replaced the beautiful soaps, creams and scents with a piece of used soap from the showers – with embedded strand of curly hair – some half-empty discount store deodorant and a grimy flannel. Then I carefully wrapped it all back up again and he never noticed. I'm assuming he gave it to his mum on Christmas Day, but I didn't have the balls to ask him how she had reacted to receiving the present.

I did a similar switch around a few years earlier when a player brought in his new mobile. He was obsessed with having the latest phones and had it delivered to the training ground as he was single and nobody would have been at home. The receptionist passed him the package. When he went training, I retrieved it and opened his phone. Taking a small strip of sellotape, I placed it across the ear piece and then clipped the front of the phone back on. He couldn't understand why everyone he tried to call sounded distant and sent back his disappointing new toy.

Our Christmas is not totally self-indulgent. One of the most humbling duties is when we are invited to local hospitals to meet poorly kids and give them presents. I am now very glad to do this, but find it heart-breaking since I have had kids of my own. When I meet kids with cancer or very severe disabilities it makes my constant small anxieties about football insignificant, and I realise how blessed I am.

When I was younger, I used to dread these visits. I'd never seen such sick children before and meeting kids wired up to tubes shocked and frightened me. Then a parent, seeing how awkward I was, dispensed some good advice, saying: 'Try to crouch down to their level when speaking to them or having photos. And speak like you'd speak to any kid – don't patronise them.'

The hospital visits can provide unintentional moments of hilarity. This year, one nine-year-old with cancer told me: 'My dad says you are not very good and should be sold but my mum says you are handsome. She fancies you.' Mum and dad, standing about two yards away, heard all this and were overcome with embarrassment.

'Tell your mum that she's right and your dad that he's wrong,' I replied, knowing that both parents could hear.

One of my three teammates accompanying me overheard this and said: 'No, tell your mum that she's wrong and your dad that he's right.'

Everyone was laughing, including the nurses, one of whom was beautiful. A teammate got her number and I think he made his own return to the hospital, albeit to the nurses' living area.

And there is also our duty to the world of football – the packed Christmas programme of matches. After the party hangovers have gone, players will knuckle down during this vital part of the season. This year, as is usual, we have four games in nine days over Christmas and the New Year. Our physio really earns his money at this time of year.

The physiotherapist performs a crucial role at a club. If you're injured then you'll be seeing him every day and often ringing him at home with updates. He provides a key part of your support network. He needs to lift you, be sympathetic to what you're going through, yet be realistic and not fill you with false hope. He needs to be firm with the manager who wants his best players playing and will be inclined to take risks on them.

More games means more injuries at Christmas, but players will want more massages. A club masseur will travel everywhere with the team. Our female masseur has left; her little indiscretion became too widely known. When I started, women masseurs were the norm, but my current manager has followed the trend and opted for a bloke as a replacement. Too much temptation, too likely to end in tears, too many stories of players sleeping with masseurs – or trying to and upsetting them.

The yoga teacher who also became a notch on the bedpost is still hanging on, for the present.

The male masseur will have all the qualifications and his massage table goes everywhere with us.

A massage will last for twenty minutes and usually focus on the area where there's tension: legs, back or neck. I like to wear compression pants too which look like tights and keep the blood moving around your legs. I wear them underneath jeans or pants, wear them for most of my life. So when I take them off to play my legs feel 'free'.

The masseur's room is next to the physio room at our

training ground. Around Christmas, the physio's room will become even busier than it usually is. A physio needs to be sociable because players congregate in his room, either for banter with the injured players when they first come in for training, or for a rub and massage. Players will see a physio to have a sore ankle strapped up, goalkeepers get their fingers strapped. If I had to choose one single hub at a football club then it would be the physio's room, with the radio on in the background and pennants from rival clubs on the wall.

The physio picks up a great deal of information in this way, about who is happy and who is not. Like the assistant manager, his loyalty is to the manager, especially if he's brought him in. The walls in the physio's room definitely have ears. And they'll hear plenty over Christmas.

If the Boxing Day game is at home, as it is this year, we'll come in an hour earlier on Christmas Day, do an hour's training and then get back to our families. If we're away, we'll eat Christmas dinner earlier, then go in later in the afternoon, do an hour's training and then travel to where we are going to play the next day. My overriding feeling about playing over the festive period is how tough it can be – it's a lot for the body to take, especially as we will play two games in just three days. Our bodies are not used to that and it's very, very hard to be 100% for the second of those three games.

Ask any pro and they'll tell you that the worst day is the day after a game. You're usually stiff from playing and tired from a lack of sleep. No one sleeps well after a match because you tend to re-run events through your mind. Getting in at 2 a.m. from an away game can play havoc with your sleep too, especially if you have young kids who will be up a few hours later.

The schedule allows no time to recover physically and we have to perform again the next day, often on frozen pitches. I don't know how the players did it years ago when they played back-to-back matches on Christmas and then Boxing Day.

Fans may look forward to the Christmas games more than others. Lower down the leagues, there tend to be more derby games over the festive period, but the preparation remains exactly the same when you are a player.

Christmas Day finds me eating half a Christmas dinner just so I can join in with my family. A Christmas dinner is actually good for you: one part protein and two parts carbohydrate, so the dieticians at the club have no problem with players eating them. I'd like to say that my kids plead with me not to leave the house, but they're lost in a world of Christmas presents and don't miss me. My wife is used to me being away. That's the life of a footballer's wife. She keeps the show on the road while I have boots and will travel.

The managers don't relax, though. They become paranoid (with good reason) that the players don't want to be missing out on all the fun and like them to be under control in hotels as much as possible, home games included.

We don't usually stay in a hotel before home games, but our manager wants us in one before this Boxing Day clash. If it gives him peace of mind then we have to respect that. He probably fears that we'll get carried away on Christmas pudding and brandy. Even then, it's difficult to control all the players all the time.

This is the one time of the year players envy their mates

with normal lives who can go out when they choose, though the odd cancelled game might allow potential for some relaxation. One Premier League team was in their hotel the night before an away game on New Year's Day. The temperature outside was minus five and there wasn't a sane person who thought the game would be on the next day. Most of the team sneaked out and had a few beers. Why not? It wasn't like they had a game to prepare for.

As they slept, temperatures rose well above zero and the previously frozen pitch gradually became playable. The game was on – to the horror of the players – yet they still fancied their chances as they were a mid-table playing a team who were really struggling at the bottom. They lost.

Not only that, the defeat started a run of terrible form which saw them slide down the table and led to the manager getting sacked. Never has the 'fail to prepare, prepare to fail' adage been so true.

We travelled to one fixture on New Year's Eve and had a pleasant meal that night in the hotel ahead of the match the following day. A few of the lads had ideas of sneaking out for a few beers – they even packed pants, shoes and a shirt – but the manager was right onto them.

After the meal, he told us that we were to go to our rooms and have a good night's sleep. He also said that he didn't trust a single one of us. The assistant manager had his eyes on a few beers too – until the manager told him to sit on a chair in the hallway of the hotel we were staying in until 3 a.m. and make sure that no players went out. He did and we didn't.

Missing out on Christmas is one of the things you sacrifice

and people are only too ready to point out that they'd happily swap shoes with you, especially given 'what you earn'.

It amuses footballers when their salaries are printed as 'per week' in the papers. It builds up an image of us going to collect an envelope stuffed with notes every Friday after training.

Players get paid monthly. The payslips are sent from the main offices at the stadium to the training ground, where the first-team coach hands them out after training. There's a chance for a bit of banter and the coach will say: 'I can't believe we're still paying you,' or, 'Not much left for you this month after all your fines.'

The money is divided into three columns, gross, tax and net. The figures on a pay-slip are mind-boggling for a Premier League footballer. The amount of tax paid each month is higher than the average man earns for a year. When you read your payslip it's remarkable to see just how much has been paid into your bank.

Appearance fees and win bonuses are all detailed, as are the huge amounts of tax deducted. Your salary will be higher in December because there are more games in December, more appearance fees, more win bonuses.

Contracts can be very complex, making a mockery of the 'per week' statements. Win bonuses are not straightforward. For one, the win bonus when you are in the top four is higher than if you are 18th – and there's a sliding scale. Same for appearance fees. They kick in after the first six games when the season has settled down. Success is rewarded in football.

The agent will get 5% of everything, not 15% as is popularly believed. So if an agent does a deal where a player gets £50,000 a week, he'll pocket £2,500 a week. Not bad for striking one deal, eh?

When you finally make it as a top-flight footballer, it is the best buzz of your life. The reality of your new situation is brought home when you open your pay packet. I made my first-team debut when I was on £60 a week. I used public transport and was always skint; walked past the clothes shop where the first-team lads shopped and dreamed of just one pair of jeans from there.

Then everything changed. The money rocketed within weeks and I was taken aback by how much the bonuses were, bonuses on top of my £60 basic deal.

To start with, a first-team appearance accrued £3,000; for my second game I received that sum and an additional £8,000 bonus because it was a Cup game and the players were on 25% of the gate receipts. Suddenly I had £10,000 burning a hole in my pocket. Within weeks, the manager called me in and told me that I was now a first-team player and should have a first-team contract. That gave me four years of stability on money I wouldn't have been able to dream of.

Within just a few months of making my debut I had £5 to 10,000 a week to spend on whatever I liked and the amount in my bank account went up and up.

I was soon in the fancy clothes shop, where I didn't just buy the jeans I wanted, but bought them in four different colours. It was very easy to get carried away and occasionally I did, like buying a yellow Versace waistcoat with a Mickey Mouse print on the front. I wore it once and was, quite rightly, slaughtered.

Money can change young footballers – a cliché, but sadly

only too true. They can became arrogant because they think they are better than other people, invincible even. A good manager will attempt to knock such traits out of them.

Most footballers of my age did three things when the money started rolling in. First off, they bought a BMW convertible with all the trimmings; second, a smart Rolex and thirdly, they paid for a boob job for their girlfriend – who was obviously delighted that her partner was now earning a fortune . . . for her to spend on surgery, shoes and clothes. Today, the newly monied will buy a Prada coat, and a £100 bottle of Jo Malone or Acqua di Parma aftershave for their new £300 washbags. A big new watch will be spotted on the wrist within weeks, a Rolex or a massive Hublot.

You can see a transformation in months. They start using Clinique moisturiser (that company were so in tune with their target audience that their rep dropped off bags of free samples for us), have £80 hair cuts rather than a budget do at the local barber's. With so much money you can see why the *Professional Player* magazine, which is sent to every member of the Professional Footballers' Association, attracts adverts like a £90,000 F1 racing simulator for the home or a £42,000 transparent pool table. There are £800 headphones and a £65,000 personal boat and submarine. They are pitching these at footballers who they think will be easily parted with their money. And plenty are.

As the money comes in, the sensible option is to buy a house and pay the mortgage off as quickly as possible. Then invest the rest wisely: buy properties, shares and try to get financial advisors who don't rip you off. Harder than it sounds.

A twenty-year-old lad doesn't know the difference between good or bad financial advice.

The reality is often very different and the money goes to many a young player's head. One took himself off to St. Tropez at the earliest opportunity and saw a bright orange Lamborghini glistening in the sun. He thought it looked like the coolest thing ever and bought the same car when he returned to England. What looked cool in the South of France in June looked ridiculous in northern England in December and he was ribbed mercilessly for it.

Another lad, who had a reputation for drinking and driving to the extent that the police had a word with the club about it, bought a private number plate for his fancy new car. That attracted even more police attention and he was arrested weeks later and charged with drink driving. He couldn't say that he hadn't been warned and his career petered out soon after.

Despite the size of the sums involved, the wad can be squandered very easily if you're not careful. I know a young lad on £15,000 a week (see, I'm as bad as the media there). He'll see half that after tax and agent commissions. He then pays £2,000 rent on a very fancy apartment, spends over a grand on a car and some ridiculous finance/insurance deal he's tied himself into. So he's not left with a huge amount. I can already see the hangers-on eyeing up the rest. He's been known to blow £20,000 on a five-day holiday to Vegas, flying first class, staying in a suite and drinking bottles of Cristal champagne. He's twenty.

I saw another player come into the money and change pretty badly. We went to a club and he fancied a girl, who had a boyfriend. He told the bouncers that the boyfriend was pestering the players and the boyfriend was ejected, when he'd done nothing wrong. The girlfriend knew nothing of this; she just couldn't find her boyfriend and stayed with her friends. The footballer moved in to chat her up by offering her top-of-the-range champagne. How can a normal lad compete with that? Then again, why would anyone want to compete with such idiotic behaviour?

I can't criticise. I saw a beautiful girl in a club one night, and would have done anything to pull her. She told me she was a nursery nurse. She knew who I was, I think.

I told her that my girlfriend was going away for a year and that we needed a carer to look after the kids. She told me that she earned £8,000 a year. I offered her £22,000 a year to look after my kids. And a car. I pulled her that night.

Four days later she turned up at my front door. She told me that she had quit her job and wanted to know when she should start. She had work references in her hand. It all started to come back to me. I lied and told her that there had been a change of plan, a problem with visas. She went back to her old job. I was an idiot, I know.

I'm not a bad lad, but I can look back at a few incidents where I cringe. A local nightclub would let me in regardless of what was on. There was never a problem; even if I was with five mates the owner would make a fuss of me. I turned up one night with fifteen drunk mates. The owner told me that I was pushing it. His club was full, it was one-in one-out and it was raining. I persuaded him and he relented. The clubbers getting wet in the queue were not happy. They would have to wait much longer. One shouted: 'I don't mind XXX getting in because he plays for XXX, but why all of his mates?'

One mate shouted back: 'Fuck off, paying public.' Horrible and arrogant, I know.

One teammate came from a top European league. He thought he was above English law. He would drink and drive, despite me telling him not to. We went out one night in his car and he decided to park in the middle of a high street where only buses were allowed.

'You can't park here,' I explained.

'Me park anywhere,' he replied.

'But you'll get a parking ticket which will cost £40 and then £80 if you don't pay it.'

He laughed at me and opened his glove box. What seemed like hundreds of parking tickets fell out.

Christmas is not a time for hitting the pub with your mates either, but if you are a top-level pro then you would not be hitting the pubs with your mates on a regular basis, anyway. By the start of January though, I'm usually gagging for a night out with friends. The problem is, they're all skint and shattered after going out too much. And all the bars are empty. I'm sure you all feel sorry for us. As you should, if you see some of the pitches we have to play on.

Despite the improvements in top-level pitches I've described, they can still be dangerous. The weather is a variable which managers can do nothing about. I've played in matches that should have been called off because the pitches were waterlogged; matches where the managers really wanted to get the game called off because they had injuries. At one club, it had been raining heavily all week and our game was in doubt. The manager wanted it to be called off and told the groundsman to put more water on the pitch ahead of a pitch inspection the day before the game. He got his wish.

Hard or frozen pitches are worse because they affect the bounce of the ball. I played at one ground outside the top division just before Christmas where I could barely stand on my feet. The final quarter of the pitch, the portion which had received no sunlight, was frozen. We'd travelled five hours by coach to play the game and that brought a pressure from us to play it, a 'we've travelled here, let's get it on' feeling which I'm sure, sub-consciously, affected the referee's mindset when he said that the game would go ahead.

I went up for a few headers and didn't land well. It really, really hurt and there was a risk of serious injury. But what was the alternative? We had fans who'd fought their way across the country. We saw them at the services on the way home, which is unusual.

Most of the time, we don't get to see the public. Teams don't stop in motorway service stations for fear of problems and the bigger teams usually fly anyway. For many domestic games, we are taken to a private terminal and board the plane straightaway. There's a company which specialises in thirty-two seater planes which a lot of the top clubs use. The players just have to get themselves to the airport, which isn't too much of a task. Or it shouldn't be.

One foreign lad went to the wrong airport, ending up at an aerodrome full of two-seater planes parked near a grass runway. He'd typed 'airport' into his satnav and the problems started when the wrong one came up.

A few weeks later, we told him that he needed a visa as we were playing a game in Wales. He believed us and panicked for a few minutes. Then we reassured him that he didn't even need a passport. One player parked his car in the drop-off zone at an airport before an away game and was surprised when his car wasn't there when he returned, having been towed away.

When you travel through public areas as a football team, you could not stand out more if you were all in fancy dress. Twenty men passing through an airport in club tracksuits is a real head turner. You get all kinds of people who don't know you approaching and asking for autographs so that they can tell their kids/grandkids that they met you. Fair enough.

It's funny as they ask the kitman and fitness people for autographs as well and the best advice to them is 'just sign', but some of the lads take advantage of the safety in numbers to take the piss with autographs in a manner they wouldn't get away with outside the ground. I was with one team who all signed the signatures of *EastEnders* actors. I wonder what little Johnny made of it when his granddad gave him a sheet with 'Ian Beale' and 'Pat Butcher' on it.

I'm on a roll this Christmas and follow our pre-party draw with one of the best performances of my career. I feel fit and confident. I have a good first five minutes – the first five minutes of a match are important in setting the template for the game and also in your own mind. My touch is glorious and everything I try comes off – though that is helped by my marker having a nightmare. The players around me raise the bar too and we win comfortably. The larger than average crowd are really charged, dressed in Christmas jumpers and a few Santa hats and the whole occasion feels incredible. My only regret is that the ninety minutes passed so quickly.

I want to enjoy the moment, have a night out and relax in the afterglow of my achievement for as long as possible.

But nothing stands still in football. We're in training in the morning as we have an away game in less than forty-eight hours.

And I am totally crap in that match. Everything that came off on Boxing Day fails. I'm substituted after sixty-seven minutes, knackered, gutted and secretly pleased to be taken off in favour of one of the subs who has had to travel and train throughout the festive period without playing. That must be a right pain in the arse, but managers like to stick with their best seven or eight players and I'm one of them, or I was until today.

I get straight back on the team bus as I'm only thinking about going home. Rather than risk airline food, we eat our meal on the team bus to the airport. The chef travels with us to away games and can use the facilities to heat up ready prepared food in the microwave, but, even so, the pasta is nice enough.

As on all team buses we have satellite television now, so we watch *Sky Sports News* and catch the scores coming in. The team buses are beautiful, with big leather chairs, tables and a settee at the back. There's a toilet, kitchen and a divider to separate the players from the manager and his staff at the front. Like today, coaches are often driven to an away stadium just to transfer the team from the airport to the team hotel and then the stadium, and then the stadium back to the airport. It seems silly, an empty coach going to the other side of the country, but then Arsenal flying to Norwich also seems stupid.

I am called up to the front by the assistant manager with

the ominous: 'The manager wants a word.' I've been half-expecting the summons. I know that I stank today.

The boss is watching a DVD of the match. He's got it in his hands already. In fact he's had it since a minute after the final whistle. And a minute before the first-half whistle, he had a two-minute highlights package handed to him by Jeff, our video analysis man. Jeff goes home and away with us and films everything. The manager briefs him on what he wants – set pieces, goals, an overview.

Jeff is also available for the players to use. Some request DVDs, like a two- or three-minute recording of every touch that they've had in the game. They find it useful, to see what they're doing right and wrong, especially if watched with a coach. Others, myself included, don't like watching games again and I especially don't like watching myself back. I might catch the highlights on *Match of the Day* if I've done well. That's it.

Today, the manager points out one of my mistakes. 'What were you doing here?' he asks. He's not angry, just frustrated that I did so well on Boxing Day and was half the player today. I blame the referee. He laughs and that dispels the tension.

Referees are a weird one for players. I once stepped off a team coach at an away ground to see the referee signing autographs outside the main entrance. My manager was right onto him.

'Caught in the act,' he shouted, 'look at the state of you, what chance do we have today when you're signing autographs for home fans?'

It was comical, though not as comical as that daft warm up referees do with their assistants, where they stride along and pretend they're fitter than they are. The autograph-signing referee was a bit embarrassed. He was probably caught between not wanting to seem rude by refusing to sign an autograph and making himself look conceited, but the incident showed how referees don't always know what their role should be.

Players don't resent referees and neither do managers, but asking them actively to respect referees is a waste of time. I walked off the pitch at Old Trafford during one game to see Sir Alex Ferguson slaughtering the referee in the tunnel. The whole tunnel filled with his voice and the ref seemed absolutely petrified. The referee had just given a penalty, which United missed. United were not playing well and Fergie accused the referee of posing because he was in charge of a game at Old Trafford. He wasn't complaining on ninety minutes after United scored three second-half goals.

I've seen managers be very harsh on referees as a deliberate tactic. An outspoken former boss of mine would lay it on thick, saying: 'People like you get people like me the sack.'

Few referees are singled out or dreaded. No player or manager thinks that a referee is genuinely biased against a certain side like some fans do. They wouldn't have reached the top as refs if they had been so obviously biased. At half-time the manager might caution: 'Watch the referee. He's not in control of the game and he needs to even things up.' Or he might use a referee to justify his own decision making. I was once told: 'I'm going to bring you off now, son, because I don't trust that ref with you. You have to trust me here because I think he's looking to send you off.' That was a clever way of deflecting an awkward decision.

However, a manager may warn that some refs are likely to give certain types of decisions. There are refs who will favour defenders or attackers, some refs who will give a foul after a fair challenge in a 50/50, others who will wave play on. A lot of referees miss what goes on because they're ball watchers. They've never played football – and I'm a big advocate of former pros training to be refs – so they watch when a goal kick is taken where there's unlikely to be an infringement, and miss the incident at the other end of the pitch.

There are also very different types of referees. The know-it-all type provides a full lecture back about the history of the rules when a player questions something.

Then there are the matey ones. The ones who'll call you by your first name and say: 'How are you? Not seen you for a while. How is life here?' Players like this. It's simple, courteous and shows them to be human.

You can tell from the fear in their eyes if the ref is one of the nervous types who will be shitting themselves, especially if they're inexperienced. Remember Andy D'Urso retreating from a raging Roy Keane et al? A confident ref would have stood his ground and said: 'If you say that again I'm going to book you.'

The headmaster type is my least favourite, the martinet who looks down on players, the one whose boots will be polished so much that he can see his face in the reflection. He'll be on a power trip and revel in his authority. He'll be the one who insists on moving the ball back seventeen centimetres at a dead ball rather than letting play flow better. He'll be out of touch with the football environment because he's only ever part of it for ninety minutes once a week. It would do no harm for refs to visit training grounds, watch training and pick up on the banter between footballers.

I could probably only name three or four referees and two of those are retired. That's how it should be; they're not the stars. I've also noticed standards improve since I've been a pro. The top refs are now very good; the ones lower down make more mistakes. When I started playing there were some comedy refs, blokes who looked like they'd just walked straight out of a pub holding a whistle. Fitness levels are better now.

I feel for referees sometimes. They are unfairly judged on their decisions by four or five 'experts' watching four or five cameras in slow motion.

Refs will make mistakes, but all you want from a ref is consistency, for them to know the game and for them not to make too many mistakes. Because when they do, it can be very costly. And I say that as a player who once missed out on promotion because of a mistake by a ref.

You find yourself to be a very popular neighbour when you're a footballer, especially at Christmas. It's a tricky one. I want to fit in with people and more importantly so does the wife, but I have constantly to be aware of potential ulterior motives. We'll pop over to a few neighbourhood parties with the kids. We don't leave them at home, as they provide the ready-made excuse should I get cornered in the kitchen by the local tactician who wants to analyse why we haven't won every game this season. Or the tipsy mum asking: 'Do you know David Beckham? What's he really like?'

I bat them away, telling the mums that Beckham is a nice

lad (he is) and play a little game back to the coach in the armchair by trying to ask him more questions about his job as an accountant than he asks me. If I can get to ten before he can then I've won. Such strategies help me – and others like me – survive.

Because you're a footballer people will be attracted to you, male and female. Ryan Giggs once advised the younger United players to be careful who they knocked about with, asking: 'Did you know them before you became a professional footballer?' If the answer was no then the inference was that they should be treated with suspicion.

It's all right for Giggs to say that, he's never moved away from home and can stay loyal to his childhood mates. That's not the reality for most players who move around from city to city. You lose touch with a lot of friends and meet new ones. Just because you met them when you are a well-known footballer doesn't make them a bad choice, but you have to be a decent judge.

When footballers move to a new city with their families naturally they look for more upmarket areas where the settled middle classes live. We're still friends with a couple we met a decade ago. They weren't particularly interested in me being a footballer, in fact the husband said: 'I hear you play football for X. I'm awfully sorry, I don't follow football. XX (a club legend) used to live around the corner though and he seemed like a nice chap.' He asked my second name twice and said that he'd mention me to a friend who did like football. I liked that.

We had children of the same age which created common ground automatically. I was glad that he wasn't into football.

DECEMBER

He loved rugby and would go and watch it live. I had little interest in rugby, but I liked his passion for it and learned a lot about it from him. As he'd never seen a game of football and had no inclination to do so, I set myself a challenge to get him to a match.

His family had helped out with our kids and we really liked them. He kept making excuses about not coming to a game, which I loved. One day, he relented and agreed to come to a home match with me. I really looked after him, decent tickets, players' lounge, lift there and back. I introduced him to a couple of players, one who later asked what the fuck my neighbour was wearing on his 'plates of meat' (feet).

I got the neighbour settled down with a match programme and left him to it. He was spotted reading the FT ten minutes before kick-off, the big pink paper spread across the space for the two neighbouring seats. I think he enjoyed himself.

I've had neighbours whom I haven't been so keen to help out. Tickets are the perennial bugbear. A neighbour knocked on my door and asked if I could get him some tickets for a forthcoming match against Manchester United. Reluctantly, I told him that I would.

Keeping my promise was not easy. A player gets six complimentary tickets and then access to buy another six, with the money deducted from your pay packet. I'm not comfortable about the comps, but some of the players couldn't care less. It's more money for them, money for nothing. At some clubs, these complimentaries have been pooled and ended up in the hands of ticket touts. The money comes back to the participants as cash. Footballers are fascinated by cash because they rarely see it. Sounds stupid? Let me explain. You get paid huge amounts, but those amounts are just numbers on a payslip. You pay for most things using a credit card. When you are handed a brick of cash then you get a childlike thrill at seeing all that folded money.

Despite the problems and the overwhelming demand from family and other acquaintances, I sorted the neighbour out with two tickets. I didn't have his phone number, but went round to his house and knocked on his door forty-eight hours before the match. He told me that he now couldn't go to the game.

Another lad asked me for tickets to an away game where they were like gold dust. I pulled a few strings and got him two tickets. I never saw any money, I think people just assume that you are rich enough not to need reimbursing.

There are other dangers if you make yourself too open.

'Can you get me an autographed shirt? Can you come and coach my kid's team on a Saturday? Can you get me a training kit? Can you come and do the presentation at my mate's Sunday League team? Can you sponsor me? Can you get a ball signed?'

There won't be a player reading this who doesn't know what I mean. You try to help people but it's impossible to deal with too many requests. And it's a little disheartening to see that an autographed ball (which cost me £30) was being used in the street by kids a few months later, the leather cutting up easily on the concrete.

You lose a little bit of faith in humanity. I used to the buy a paper each morning and see the same miserable fella in the newsagents. He didn't pay any attention to me. One day, he decided that he wanted to be my best mate.

Or the neighbour whom I quite liked . . . until details of

our conversations appeared on an internet forum word-for-word. I was told about that by the press officer at the club who monitors such things. I felt there had been a breach of trust, but it was a valuable lesson too – a still tongue makes for a wise head.

Another year nearly over. I'm not at any New Year's Eve parties, sidestepping eager neighbours as I'm away in another hotel. We're mid-table and satisfied with that. We're holding steady in the league. We're still in the FA Cup – though that's because our first match is in the 3rd round next week. But first, another game tomorrow.

January

For the first weekend in January we've been drawn away to a tiny club in the FA Cup 3rd round. Their ground holds 6,000, which is less than one of the stands behind our goal. The media have been in overdrive, with all the focus on the minnows.

We were given two days off after the game on New Year's Day. I needed them after four games in ten days. I managed the night out I was so desperate for, hooking up with a few old friends on January 2nd, though most of them went home early, too hungover and skint to have any enthusiasm, just as predicted. I had a meal with my wife one night; she was far better company.

The FA Cup is not the big deal it was. The Premier League is a much, much bigger deal. Why? Money. A club receives a million or two for winning the FA Cup, it gets £60 million from its television contract with the Premier League. So it's £60 million or £2 million. Not difficult.

JANUARY

Does a club always have to choose between Premier League and Cup? If you're a middle-ranking team like we are this season, then, yes. Say we get to the FA Cup 6th round. That's four games. Four games in which we're likely to pick up injuries and suspensions which would directly affect our league campaign. We lost one of our best players last season, a key central midfielder, through an injury in an FA Cup match. For one month, our team was 10% weaker for his absence. We were eliminated in the next round.

This is why Premier League teams field weaker sides in the early stages of the FA Cup. It seems wrong to someone who grew up watching the hours of build up before the FA Cup final on the TV, but it's about money. Our contracts now contain a clause that we earn 40% less should we play outside the Premier League, that's 40% less basic and appearance money.

Would we prefer full wages or a reasonable Cup run? Full wages. Would we prefer good wages or to win the FA Cup? I'd probably say the latter, but others would argue there is little chance of winning it.

Lower league clubs see the FA Cup differently. I've seen both sides and been at a club when they drew a top side away. The first thing the chairman said was: 'That's half a million quid for us' – equivalent to about half the playing budget for the whole season. It's an even bigger deal for non-league clubs. The non-league side in the town near to where I live had a brief adventure in the FA Cup which energised the whole place. They usually get crowds of 200, but had over 1,000 by the 4th qualifying round. Their little Cup run brought in £50,000, most of it in prize money from the FA. That was enough to run the club for a year.

The prize money increases each round, but it's small fry to the biggest clubs. The players get 25% of the prize money, so we received £700 each after winning a 3rd round tie last season. A packet when you earn a grand a week in League Two, not so much when you earn £30,000. And not so much when you get to share £3 million in the players' pool if you stay in the Premier League.

But I still love the FA Cup and it's my contention that it represents a realistic chance of a trip to Wembley, although I'm in the minority in my current dressing room. Look at the teams who've reached the semi-finals in recent years, there are always a few middle-ranking teams and even teams from outside the Premier League.

When you're a club like us, you don't want a tricky away tie at a lower league club. Play away at a Rochdale or Southend and the tie is set up for you to fail. It will probably be televised and almost everyone watching will want you to lose. People's natural inclination is to support the underdog, to hope for a giant killing. I'm exactly the same, but it's different when you are the giant.

The manager will say to us before the match: 'There will be some shocks in the Cup today, make sure you're not one of them.' The problem is that if we're resting half of our team then there's every chance that there will be a shock.

And that's why I'm a bit edgy today. I've been told that I'm playing and we're putting quite a strong team out. We prepare for the match as usual, staying in a five-star hotel we use for league games in the area. The advantage of that is that we're familiar with the hotel. We know it's a good place and one player has become familiar with a member of the staff on previous visits, so he's happy, especially when she sneaks into his room after finishing work in the hotel spa.

The disadvantage is that the autograph collectors know you're there. That's not kids, but the scruffy fuckers who have got books and books of stuff which they want signing. They've not visited a dentist in their lives; they look no different to the trainspotters at Crewe Station. Maybe I'm being harsh. Maybe they are harmless, but I know that some of them are professional autograph dealers and it all feels a bit grubby that they are profiting from selling my signature.

One of our coaches has arranged to meet a merchandise seller. The coach was a big-name forward in the eighties. Won everything there is to win and never got more than £2,000 a week for his efforts. The seller pays him £600 for thirty minutes of signing memorabilia such as old programmes and shirts. I watch him and see that he's enjoying looking at the memorabilia, if not the actual pen-wielding. 'I'd do anything to do all this again,' he says. I think he means play all the games again, rather than sign autographs.

One of our players is from the town where we are playing and it's a big deal for him. He's been in demand from the local media and thinks nothing of it when he gets a call from 'Ivan Smith' at a nearby paper wanting a few words ahead of the game. We're supposed to clear any media requests with the press officer first, but the player has been told that he can do what he likes this week; good PR for the club to have him seen to be co-operating with his former local media.

Mr Smith informs the player that he will get a hero's reception and tells him that the fans have had a banner made in his honour with the word 'legend' on it. The player likes to hear all this. A few hours later, someone (me) leaves a pillow case with the word 'legend' on it in marker pen. I left it in the corridor outside his hotel room, knocked on the door and ran off. I think he was a bit confused by it all.

You need to lighten the mood sometimes and there are a few tricks of the trade for idiots like me. Television remote controls work for all the televisions in a hotel and if you stay on the ground floor you can creep outside the other rooms and control the volume through any gaps in the windows. A player might be dozing and he'll have the shock of his life as he suddenly has an African channel turned up to full volume – with no idea why.

Tonight, I room with my usual roommate. We have similar habits, like the room to be quiet so that we can read a magazine or watch a film on the iPad rather than the hotel television. We like to go to bed at the same time, around eleven. He has no annoying habits. My worst roommate was a player who smoked. He didn't do it in the room, but would play cards with a couple of other players until 1a.m. and then come back to the room, fumbling about to get in the door, waking me up and stinking of fag smoke. Another roommate was never off the phone to his Mrs. It did my head in as neither of them would put the phone down without being the last one to say: 'I love you.' They'd spend ten minutes ending the conversation. Another roomie would ask his girlfriend to put the dog on the phone and then speak to his dog. I could hear his mutt barking away. He didn't appreciate my advice to get professional help.

Match day starts as normal. Our team coach is escorted from hotel to the ground by two police motorcyclists. We used to have our own coach, but now use a specialist company who supply coaches for other Premier League teams. They personalise the coach for whichever team uses it by putting on headrests with your club badge. There's nothing on the outside which shows it's you and it's probably better not to bring attention to yourself. The coach driver can do without rival fans beeping, giving the vees and throwing a beer can as he's doing sixty on the motorway.

The coach normally parks very close to the stadium or even inside. Not today. We turn past a pub, whose forecourt is full of home fans who know who we are. Who else could we be? We get a mixture of two-finger salutes, applause and stares from awestruck locals as they try to scan for our more famous players. Difficult as the glass is tinted. I've been on a team bus when an idiot has thrown a brick through a window before a derby match, but there's no real aggression today. All 6,000 tickets have been sold, 1,500 to our travelling fans. Of the 4,500 home fans, 2,000 of them will be glory hunters who never usually go to games. I pay attention to things like that because I've always considered myself a fan too. Other players don't notice and, if they do, they don't care. But I genuinely appreciate it if someone travels the length of the country to watch me play football. My mates from home do it, and I know what it takes. I would have been doing it with them had I not made it as a pro.

There are placards from the local paper posted on every lamppost. 'Read all about the big Cup game tomorrow,' they say. It's their biggest match in decades, probably the biggest thing to happen in the town for years, too.

'Poor in-bred bastards,' says the South Londoner who

hadn't left the capital until he started playing football at a decent level. 'I bet they fucking hate people like us.'

The coach stops by a temporary burger van selling rancid food we'd never be able to eat behind one end of the tiny stadium and we have to walk the rest of the way. We pass through a corner gate and go along a small strip of terracing by the side of the pitch to the ageing main stand. Barely above zero and the club tracksuit isn't enough to keep us warm even on that short hike. My ears sting, though some of the other players don't get that as theirs are covered by £600 earphones the size of small footballs. Personally, I can't tell the difference in the sound between the mini white Apple ones and the big expensive ones. But then I can't tell the difference between a good and a bad wine either.

I look at the pitch, but I'm distracted by a man who appears to be working with the ground staff. He's gesticulating and saying something which we can't understand. I get the impression he's swearing. A kindly club official tells us to ignore him and explains that he's a local 'character' who has been going to matches and 'helping out' for sixty years. He also explains that he was a steward for years, but they had to take his fluorescent bib off him after he was clocked throwing a snowball at the Boston United goalkeeper. So now he watches the grass grow and tries to intimidate opponents.

Looking at the state of the pitch, I'm not sure his attention has done much for the grass's health and vitality. One half seems to be comprised of sand, the other has a sparse bit of green growth on it. We can laugh, but it will make it difficult for us.

Some players fancy games like this, some don't. The

manager needs to use his head and pick the right players. The dressing rooms are minute and the manager goes into 'war' mode in the cramped confines when the doors are shut.

'The changing rooms are too small. Just the starting eleven and three subs in here first, the rest can get changed after,' he begins.

Then he barks: 'Get the excuses out of the way now. We know the pitch is shit. We know it's freezing. We know the three showers are crap and there are no baths. We know their number four is a clumsy fucker who is going to try and kick lumps out of you. We know the referee is going to give us nothing. We know their players are shit.'

'Well one of two of these can play,' interrupts the first-team coach, pointing at us. That brings laughs.

We're invited to add to the list.

'1970s tannoy playing Wham,' chips in one.

'Shit club badge,' another.

'Shit town full of weirdos.'

'I don't want to be here,' admits our winger, while pulling a puppy dog face.

'Shit manager for the away team,' ends the litany. The manager laughs, the mood is good as we get changed. Then, after the warm ups when the home fans ask us to sign their £3 'FA Cup special match programme' we pass down a tunnel so narrow that there's only space for one player at a time, then through a cage where you can smell the Bovril and pies on the breath of the fans standing on the terracing on either side.

We run out and watch the fans throw bits of paper in the air as if it's going to make any difference whatsoever. They go wild again when the local heroes have a shot which goes thirty yards wide. Then we put four or five past them. There's no showboating, no piss-taking. They're the lowest rung of professional footballers who have done well to reach the FA Cup 3rd round.

We respected them and they weren't humiliated because they gave us a decent game. No one tried to make a point, there were no grudges, no over-the-top tackles. They were an honest bunch. We just had more quality, players who can finish half chances. That's why we are paid £40,000 a week and not £400. One of the home players runs straight to me to ask to swap shirts and I'm honoured – that doesn't happen much. I tell him that it will be a pleasure and it will, until I see that I've been deducted £35 for an away shirt on my next pay roll. It has happened before.

They do their lap of honour and the local celebrity who was famous in the eighties is on the seventies tannoy saying 'well done' in his comedy accent to the players. He then tries to shake hands with all of us as we leave the pitch.

Back in the dressing room, the manager says: 'Job well done.' He wants to get out of town as soon as possible. Don't we all?

The mood eases further on the coach after the match, where one player found one of his expensive Havaianas flip-flops had been nicked from under his seat. Next thing, someone puts cheese on it and places it in the microwave for thirty seconds, ruining it. He was pissed off, but took revenge by throwing the miscreant's trainers out of the skylight. Both were reduced to wearing budget club flip-flops for the rest of the way home.

A few fans go past too, scarves out of the window in the dark and beeping us. I can remember being the kid in a car with my dad and going past a team coach.

After the draw for the next round is made (a Championship team at home in three weeks), attention switches straight back to the league. We're 12th and the season is going well for me personally, I've even scored a few good goals. The reason you play football is to score goals, or, as one manager told me, 'A team defends so it can attack.'

When you do score it's a wonderful feeling for the individual and (usually) the rest of the team. My first professional goal is up there with the best two or three memories from my career. The goal proved that I could score at the top level and boosted my confidence. A senior pro teammate could see how happy I was and got me the match ball. Unlike the other mementoes which I've stupidly given away to people who mither you for such stuff all the time, I've still got it.

A goal can change a game, change a season, change a player's fortunes. It can be the difference between a manager being under pressure and the manager having his name sung. All because of one kick or header.

Regardless of how they are scored, some goals matter more than others. A winning goal in a tight away match fifteen minutes from time gives you a far bigger high than the third in a 4–0 home win. The buzz is so pure when you run to the crowd and see 3,000 travelling fans going crazy because of what you've done. You only pick out the first row or two – and maybe only a face or two from those rows – but you feel a real unity with fans.

Goals are a reward for the team's efforts, though not all

players see it that way. Watch the way a team celebrates a goal to judge how popular a player is. When an unassuming Steady Eddy defender gets his once-every-three-years goal, then the whole team will be made up for him. If it's an egotistical player who thinks he's carrying the team, the mood will be different. The best goals are not the obvious thirty-five-yard volleys either, but team efforts which are finished when it seems technically difficult, when everything has to come together in a split second. A ball coming across your body at pace is far harder to control and score from than a loose clearance falling out of the sky.

Goals change players. I've seen a lack of goals affect a player's demeanour, seen previously confident strikers withdraw into their shell because they're not scoring. I saw a famous coach grab a non-scoring forward who kept putting his arms in the air after missing chances in training and say: 'You don't see Alan Shearer put his arms in the air when he misses. No, he puffs his chest out. Don't show disappointment, show determination like Shearer.'

Conversely, I've seen what goals can do to lift someone to feel like they're on top of the world, the centre of attention. I even saw one striker buy a new wardrobe befitting his self-acclaimed status as the main man.

Life is black and white if you're a goalscorer. You're either scoring or not, a hero or a villain. You can have steady full-backs who get a 7 every week, but there's no such thing as a steady goalscorer unless you are Messi or Ronaldo and score every week. More is expected of a forward and that's why they're usually the best paid in the team.

Confidence is a huge issue for a goalscorer and they tend

to go missing in games when it's low. They hide, rather than hog the ball – and they're greedier when they're doing well because they think they can score all the time. They can become arrogant, egotistical and so greedy it causes arguments.

One teammate was on a first ever hat-trick as we led 4–0 in one game. We got a penalty and the team wanted him to take it, but the top scorer insisted that he did. He duly scored, but the rest of the team blanked him for a week. I could see both sides of that one.

Players hate it when a goalscorer points to his name and number on his back after scoring too. It's a team game not a 'me' game and nobody likes to be seen celebrating with a name pointer. Yet no matter what you think of a player, you'd never be unprofessional enough not to give him the ball, to over-hit a pass to him or ignore him. That doesn't happen.

And although he'll never admit it, a forward hates it when he's dropped and his replacement scores. Grudges can develop which can extend to wives and girlfriends. One girlfriend was upset that her man had been dropped and replaced by another, a fact not helped by the gobby partner of the chosen player wanting the world to know how great he was for scoring in the players' lounge after. She took her revenge by keying the car of the goalscorer and his cocky girl in the car park after the game. She never did get found out.

Goals are for a team, but they're also personal. You can score and have a good game and feel good. Even if you lose. I don't like losing and I've yet to meet a professional who does, but if I've worked hard and done well, then I'm entitled to feel satisfied.

I once scored two goals in a defeat to the Premier League champions away from home. I played well, so did the team, but we were undone by a moment of genius.

Losing was momentarily unpleasant, but to be perfectly honest, I was buzzing after the game and soon forgot the result. I'd performed against the best team in the league, in front of millions watching on television. I was feeling confident about my game, my hard work was paying off. I knew people would be talking about me in the papers and that interest in me would increase. And it did.

My manager was devastated to lose, yet he was really pleased for me after the match. It was possible for him to feel two conflicting emotions, because, contrary to how some fans think, winning and losing is not a black and white issue.

I boarded the coach after the game and tried to hide my smile. Being caught smiling after your team have lost is a big no. Someone will see you and before you know it, there will be posts on the internet about how you'd been seen laughing.

I was on a high, though, and couldn't wait to watch the highlights on television as my phone buzzed with 'well played' messages. There was one from a former manager. I was completely elated.

I would never have revealed on television how good I was feeling because that's not the done thing. You're supposed to talk in clichés about how it's all about the team, yet it's not all about the team when you're a player.

How would you feel if you worked for a big company and they announced that they were losing money on the same day that you were awarded a big promotion? Would you be upset for the company or pleased for yourself?

Footballers have to think for themselves because they have such a short career and they need to make the most of it. You can't take your medals down to the supermarket to buy food, you need money.

Lionel Messi aside, there's only so much one player can do to affect a game. So, if you do well, you've done your job. And if you do your job well you get a new contract or a bigger move. When these are awarded, they are given to individuals, not to a team. You have to look after your own individual interests.

Another time you'd not be too despondent if the team lost is when you don't get picked. When I started playing, fourteen or fifteen players would travel to matches. Now it's twenty, of which eighteen are involved on the match day. Being one of the two players who doesn't even get changed is horrible. You travel in case of illness or unexpected injury, but you feel like a failure on a wasted journey.

I was once dropped for an away game at Sunderland. I played for a southern team and went all that way for nothing. We travelled by train; when you travel by coach the dropped lads are supposed to make the brews. The gaffer will say it's all about team spirit. It's also your job and you have to be professional enough to realise that someone could get ill.

I sat in the stand and home fans spotted me and asked: 'Why are you not playing today? Injured or dropped?' It's a normal question to them, but it's like they're asking for confirmation that you're a failure.

We drew that game and the lad who replaced me did well. That didn't put me in the best of moods and when the gaffer rewarded us with a night out, I stayed in the team hotel.

Had he played badly, I would have probably gone out and celebrated.

Not being involved changes how you think. You can become bitter and tension builds, occasionally exploding. For one Christmas dinner, we had to buy a named teammate a present that was relevant to him. One lad had to buy a present for the player whose place in the team he'd taken. He wrapped up a copy of the fixtures for the reserve team.

'Suppose you think that's funny do you?' said the recipient, not seeing the joke at all, as you wouldn't if your livelihood was at stake, 'I hope you break your leg.'

The weather is unremittingly awful this January, as usual. Postponed matches are a pain, they break the rhythm, leading to a loss of match fitness. A friendly match may be arranged behind closed doors to counter it. The same would happen if there was a midwinter break. We've got to keep playing. We've had a friendly arranged against another Premier League team, who, while they're not direct rivals, are at our level, just two places above us in the league. The advantage for both managers and players is that you get a game against a top-standard opponent to keep your match sharpness.

When they arrive at our training ground, one of our teammates tells us that he's going to get even with a rival he had a dispute with when the sides last met. I tell him to let it go but he ignores me. Twenty minutes into the game, our player does a terrible two-footed challenge on the rival. He's a cynical bastard and knows that he has a higher chance of getting away with it because there are no TV cameras, no photographers and no fans. As the opponent spins over on the ground in pain, their manager quite rightly goes mad.

Ours does the same. Players on both sides think that the nutter alongside me is an idiot and they're right. Yet that same nutter is so driven that he'll never give up and win us points that we wouldn't otherwise get. Pros and cons.

The nutter is taken off, while the rival is tended to by both club doctors for heavy bruising to his ankle. He was lucky that it wasn't his ankle ligaments.

Once, at another club, our manager was so fuming with us that he arranged a behind-closed-doors friendly during a cold snap in Ireland. He knew that we'd hate the idea of going, and we did. He didn't even travel himself. We played a top-level Irish side who were as good as a top non-league side in England. The pitch was dire and we didn't even win. It was his way of sticking two fingers up to the whole team and because he was secure in his position, he could and did.

Warm weather training is different. And pre-season tours and mid-season breaks are different, the latter only usually happening if you've been knocked out of the FA Cup in the 3rd or 4th round, though you can often sneak three or four days in January.

Dubai or Qatar has become the favourite destinations for Premier League teams, replacing the Canaries and Spain or Portugal where the weather can still be cool.

The team will usually go on a regular chartered or scheduled flight alongside members of the public. The mood is good beforehand, both because there will be no serious games and the prospect of a few nights out. As I've said already, I looked forward to them when I was younger, now I'd prefer not to go on them. I spend enough of my life travelling and would rather be at home with family than having my socks cut up in La Manga. But, if we do go, then we'll want a good time.

There will usually be a day-long argument between the players who want three or four agreed nights out and the manager who doesn't want the players out drinking at all. A compromise is usually reached and the last night of the trip is usually a free one.

They'll always be a few fans who happen to be spending their holiday in the same place as the team they love. You should see their faces light up as they get their wives to take photos.

At a training ground you can get away with saying hello, shake hands and pose for a picture. On a trip, some fans expect you to become their best mates and meet them in the hotel bar each night because you can't wait to discuss past matches. Sadly, I don't share their enthusiasm for one-way conversations. If I meet someone new then I'd rather not talk about football and learn something about them rather than talk about games I've played in.

The mood is laddish on these trips. I once saw a player wrap himself up in cling film, stick a baggage tag to himself and sit on the carousel for ten minutes. He went around it four times and other passengers, business types, were asking if he was OK. He was, though he'd drunk five cans of lager on the plane. He did that knowing that the manager had already gone through the airport to meet representatives of the other club.

I've seen other horseplay on a plane, like the player who grabbed the microphone and announced that the plane was going to crash. There was bedlam for two minutes until the air stewardess calmed everyone down and explained what had happened. If he did that nowadays, he'd go to jail.

As would the three players – all of them huge names – who smoked on a long-haul flight on the way back from Asia.

And after a big night out on the final night of one pre-season tour, we boarded a charter flight full of holiday-makers. Most of the players had not been to sleep and two of them were having a fart competition, to see who could produce the worst smell. The stench was awful after a night on the beer and the middle-aged couple in front were appalled. The lady turned round and begged: 'Please stop. It's like you're having a competition.' Which they were.

Her plea fell on deaf ears, however, and when the trolley came past, one of the players squeezed by it – and dropped a load of guff in the direction of the complainer's face. I cringed as her husband comforted her, reassuring her that they'd soon be home, that the rest of their holiday had been good.

Sometimes, rarely, such trips can go badly wrong. An ex-teammate was in the party of Leicester players who were charged with rape in La Manga in 2004. They went out there for a week's training and half the team ended up behind bars after three prostitutes falsely accused them of rape.

His family saw him on the news, branded a rapist even though he'd done nothing wrong. It was their nightmare, their chairman's nightmare and their manager's nightmare. They weren't guilty and none of them were charged, but they suffered imprisonment without access to the outside world for several days and considerable mental anguish.

The constant leg-pulling and juvenile behaviour is, and I

know many will disagree with me, essential to lighten the mood. I think that almost all players appreciate that they are fortunate to do what they do. If ever a player asks one of the coaches for the time, he always replies: 'Time of your life, son. It doesn't get any better than this.' He knows, he's been there and done that and wants to remind us to enjoy it, yet not everyone does enjoy it. Some footballers have real problems.

Depression, for example, is not something football deals with easily. I've seen the leaflets from the PFA and the hotlines you can ring. That's all very noble, but if a player told his teammates that he was suffering from depression, then he'd be labelled an oddball, a loner or, quite frankly, a weirdo. Some players would even delight in walking past him and making daft noises to mess with his head. Trust me, I've seen it happen.

Depression is seen as a sign of weakness and a player diagnosed with it can quickly kiss goodbye to his first-team place, because the perception is that you can't perform on a Saturday if 'your head is not right'.

So players stay silent. If they don't, they can't always rely on the person they talk to. A former teammate told the club doctor that he was feeling depressed. He thought that he was speaking in confidence, yet three weeks later his manager called him in and told him that he wouldn't be offering him a new contract and that he could look for another club. I'm sure the two conversations were related.

If a normal person goes to the doctor with depression then Prozac, or another anti-depressant will often be prescribed. This drug can't be given to footballers. Not that it is a banned performance-enhancing stimulant, rather it would actually slow down your responses and affect your performances. Or, as another club doctor put it, 'It turns you into a zombie and zombies don't win matches.'

Many players do suffer from depression, to a degree. I know one lad who appeared to have the world at his feet. He was at a big club and represented his country at Under-21 level. He got a few injuries and simply stopped enjoying his job. This went on for a while and he couldn't see the light at the end of the tunnel. One day, he just decided to jack it in and join the Barmy Army and watch England play cricket. It was a decision he didn't regret.

An Irish lad I played with decided that he'd had enough too. He wasn't enjoying being a footballer so he quit and moved back home. Irish players, particularly, seem to suffer from homesickness.

I see many older players start to have serious worries about what they are going to do when their career is over. Footballers will tell you that they can't wait to retire so that they can do the things they haven't been able to enjoy because of the demands of professional football – go skiing, go out with their mates at Christmas, go on holiday whenever they want. The reality, from what I've seen, is very different and can hit them very, very hard. Football has been the main part of their life, giving it a pattern and a schedule, and then it suddenly stops. Only very strong characters are able to deal with that. I hear stories of former players getting into a mess as they struggle to fill the days. Some turn to drugs and drink. Drink often masks depression, but it's alright to be known as a lad who can handle the beer isn't it?

Another mate whose career is winding down went to see his former club doctor. His life was in a bit of a spin because of his personal circumstances. He'd lost weight and was struggling to get out of bed in the morning, struggling to take a shower. In short, he was showing the classic symptoms of depression.

This club doctor he trusted recommended someone who had dealt with many recently retired sports people. My mate went to see him and wanted to keep it private. He was told that it would be £375 for the consultation. He stressed that he didn't want the invoice to be sent to his house because his wife would see it and he wanted to work through any issues himself.

The invoice was inevitably sent to his home address and his wife duly opened it. She went mad and accused him of living a lie. The lad did sort himself out, thankfully.

The problems encountered by finishing players take various forms. One minute they receive enormous adulation, the buzz of appearing before thousands, then nothing. The divorce rate among recently retired footballers is scandalously high. Their wives take the brunt and yet the public can't relate to it at all.

They think your life must be wonderful because you got paid a lot of money to play football, because you were young, fit and famous. They honestly have no idea of the reality.

Ironically, the best way is probably to come clean like Stan Collymore has done – and get leathered for it in some quarters. Get your problems in the open and seek professional help. That way, people will understand and be sympathetic, even if your teammates won't in football's harsh, dog-eat-dog environment.

There's now talk of Wembley after we win our FA Cup 4th round tie against the Championship side with a 2–0 victory. The Wembley dream lasts for a day until we see that we've drawn one of the best teams in the country at home in the 5th round. That's a shame because I wouldn't mind a trophy. Most footballers don't win them after becoming professionals. But, in the words of one manager: 'Every payslip is a trophy. You're very fortunate to make a living playing football, the top 1%.' He has a point.

I won my first trophy aged seven for being player of the year at my junior football club. I won it every year after that, the first of fifty or sixty trophies which I still have. Somewhere.

I started playing football at four. My dad had been a good junior footballer and my brother liked playing football a bit with his mates, but that's it. My parents tell me that that's all I did, that I had no interest in computer games or playing any other type of games apart from football.

I played in the garden until it was dark and then in the lounge with a sponge ball. The lounge was big and so it felt like a five-a-side pitch, with just me playing. I was fortunate to be bigger than the other kids and by the time I started school and playing football in the playground, I quickly realised that I was the best by a distance. That may sound arrogant, but it's the truth. At five I was better than the seven-year-olds. At seven, I was better than the ten-year-olds.

When I played for my primary school, my teacher used to

put me in net – that was after I scored eleven goals in a 12–1 win against a rival school. I got told off for taking the ball out of the area while in net. And, when I kicked the ball towards the opposition goal on the tiny pitch and it nearly went in, the teacher told me that I had to throw it rather than kick it. They wanted to hold me back. To them it was about taking part, to me it was about scoring goals and pretending that I was Maradona.

When I went to secondary school, I had to wind it in a bit. At eleven, I found that I could dribble around the thirteen-year-olds. Easily. I was accused of being a show off. The primary–school teammates who saw me as their game-winning hero were replaced by lads who saw me as a threat. I started to pass more for the school team (I was played two years above my age group) but in the playground would play three versus twenty. Me and the two other best players. Looking back, it was superb practice for developing my tech-nique because I was surrounded by people who wanted the ball which I didn't want to lose. I'd use every legal part of my body to help me.

Being good at football makes you popular, popular with the boys and the girls, though I was too interested in playing to pay too much attention to girls. I wasn't a football geek, but when my mates were going to the park and trying cider and cigarettes, I was training or playing football in a field near our house. I'll never forget a man having a word with my mum at the shops.

'I watch your son every night through my back window,' he said. 'I'm not even a big football fan, but it's a joy watching that lad. I'm sure I'll see him on *Match of the Day*.'

At thirteen, my teacher rang the local top-flight football club to say that they had a very good player. He'd done that before. The club said they'd try and get someone down to have a look at me, but apparently there was a wariness because they get such calls every day. I only found all this out years later, but the club didn't send anyone. A scout who was linked to the club spotted me and contact came that way. The club then asked the teacher why he hadn't told them about me. Some good footballers slip the net, but most don't, because they keep on attracting attention until someone does something about it.

At fourteen, I signed schoolboy forms and would travel twice a week to the Premier League club, once to train and once to play on a Sunday. Again, without sounding arrogant, I was still the best player. We'd play other Premier League clubs and I was better than the other boys, though the gap was closing and there were one or two who were as good as me. I wanted to be a footballer and did everything I could to improve the chances of that happening.

At sixteen, I had trials for England Schoolboys. I did well and just missed out on the final cut. That was the first time that I saw players who were as good as me. The news, delivered by letter, was the first rejection I'd had in my life. I was devastated and cried in my room for an hour until my dad came up and told me not to worry and that I could still be a footballer.

I knew that there were some very talented players at my age though. One, who was at Man United, was far better than me. He was like Cristiano Ronaldo, so strong, quick and technically good, but he never made it in the first team. Another at the same club, who wasn't nearly as good to my untrained eye, made it.

My school reports were always the same: 'If X paid as much attention to his school work as he does to his football then he'd be top of the class.' My concentration was all on football and anything which harmed that dream upset me. Injury or defeat would reduce the juvenile me to tears.

My progress continued. Apprenticeship, full professional contract, loans, first-team debut, international debut, the lot. The progression is gradual, there's no real moment where you think: 'I've made it', but there are 'wow' moments along the way such as your first-team debut, the first time you play for your country or the first time you play in front of a packed crowd at Old Trafford. They are the times when you think 'this is special', but the feeling doesn't last long as there's always another challenge.

As January comes to a close, there are plenty more challenges for us this season, but we'll have the help of a new signing. There have been rumours in the media for a week or two, rumours which turned out to be correct.

Nothing is confirmed until the manager walks into the training-ground dressing room one morning with a man behind him wearing distressed jeans and white Prada Sport trainers.

'This is X,' he says. 'He'll be signing for us later today. I want you to make him welcome. He can help us become a better team and push on.'

We all shake his hand and either say 'welcome' or 'all the best'. He says 'thanks' each time. We've heard good things about him as a player and a person and the manager is right, he can improve us.

JANUARY

A few hours later, we see him being unveiled on *Sky Sports News*, this time wearing a suit. He's signed a two-and-a-half-year contract. He'll be on good money, among the best in the squad, and he'll be needed straightaway and I'm pleased the club have signed him. He doesn't play in my position. On the last day of the month we travel to another away game on a Friday, where we stay in another hotel the night before the game. The routine is the same and we're to eat an evening meal at 6 p.m. We don't eat in the public area of the hotel, but in a side room normally used for functions. That's normal. The room is laid out for us to eat, there's a TV on in the corner and the massage man even sets up his table in there.

The food is to order. Our dietician has sent a list through a couple of days earlier. We're regulars at this hotel, so the chef understands what we want. We don't always get that. At one hotel, the chef apologised for the lack of pasta. Our dietician was fuming.

Tonight we eat the usual, chicken, pasta and fish, washed down with water or a cordial. Definitely no fizzy or isotonic drinks. And we return to the same room at 9 p.m. for another meal. This is normal, only this time the meal is loaded with carbohydrates – cereals, pastries, muffins and more water or a cup of tea. The extra nervous energy which you burn off needs more fuel. My heartbeat goes up by ten beats per minute in the eighteen hours leading up to a game.

The manager is absent. We seize our chance.

'Oi, noodle head,' shouts the cheekiest teammate to our new signing. The player doesn't know that he's called 'noodle head' (and he's probably only called that because he's one of the few players without very short hair), but he realises it means him.

'Every new player at this club must stand on a chair and sing a song in front of the rest of the team. Welcome to the club!'

'Please, no,' the new signing begs.

'No such thing as no at this club,' replies the player, who is also the vice-captain. 'Sing for the boys. Now!'

The player sheepishly stands on his chair and delivers a cracking rendition of a song that's clearly close to his heart. . . . *Waterloo* by Abba. It's really good, he's clearly done it in a Scandinavian karaoke competition before. He is rewarded by applause – and a barrage of bread rolls. One catches him square on the left eye, which starts to puff up. It's time for bed. Or it will be if the manager spots it.

February

Why would any village hold its annual fayre in February? That's something you need to ask the organisers of the village near to my home. They've invited me to be the special guest. How can I say no?

The organiser, a well-intentioned, community-minded, eccentric man in his sixties, turned up at my house five months ago. I didn't know him, but I agreed to turn up a) because it seemed ages away b) I felt I should and c) because I wanted to get rid of him as I was enjoying an episode of *The Wire*.

Five months on and today is the day. My wife laughs at what I've got myself into. I hoped that we'd have a fixture organised which would provide me with my perfect get-out clause; it's on a Saturday after all and I did explain that to the organiser when he door-stepped me.

We were due to play at home and there's no way that my

manager would have let me open a village fete hours before the match, no matter what the organiser thinks. And here's what the organiser thinks: that football games kick off at three, so I can pop down for an hour at twelve, say a few words and then be at the stadium in time for kick-off. If only football was so simple.

We're still at home, but we're in the FA Cup 5th round and our game, against the league champions, has been switched to Sunday afternoon for live television. That means we do light training on Saturday morning then we have a few hours free, then we meet at a hotel. The few free hours should be spent with my family; instead they fall exactly in line with the village fayre.

It's raining when I arrive. There's nowhere to park my car because the organiser seems to have fixed parking for himself and his immediate family and nobody else. There are hand-written signs saying 'organiser' on the six places outside the village hall. I smell a farce.

Half of the fayre is inside the hall, but there's a beer tent outside which is selling mulled wine and has reindeer decorations above the bar. In February. There's also an HGV which doubles up as a stage. In the middle of the HGV stands the very proud organiser, beaming. He's the DJ, the centre of attention, which is exactly how he likes it. There are perhaps a hundred people inside the village hall and thirty outside, none of them near the optimistically installed crush barriers in front of the HGV.

I walk towards the only person I know – mine host – and a little piece of me dies inside with every step. He sees me and says the following:

'Our special guest, the international footballer XX, has arrived, ladies and gentleman. He's over there in the tracksuit and the white sneakers.'

Who the fuck says 'sneakers'?

Thirty people stare at me. I haven't got a clue what to do. It's a scene straight out of Alan Partridge, with me as the fall guy.

The DJ/organiser is wearing Bermuda shorts and a Hawaiian shirt. He refuses to let the weather put a dampener on his event (even though it is). *Yellow Submarine* by the Beatles was playing when I arrived, but he replaces it with *Football's Coming Home* before jumping down off the HGV to greet me.

'Thanks for coming,' he says, 'we really appreciate it. We'll have a little chat after this song and then I'll introduce you to a few people like Ron whose company owns this trailer and Joan who is in charge of the craft stall.'

I tell him that I can't stay for too long as we have a big game tomorrow, but that I'm glad to be there. I'm not. I've brought my son and even he's embarrassed, for him and for me.

Football's Coming Home comes to a close and this is what thirty people, most of them drinking mulled wine in a covered beer tent, hear.

'Three lions on my shirt,' says the organiser. 'A warm hand please, ladies and gentlemen, for our special guest, international footballer XX.'

Five people clap, the rest stare.

'So tell us X, are X going to win the FA Cup this year? There's a big game tomorrow . . .'

I'm prepared for this and have an appropriately bland response ready. 'We'll give it our best shot. It will be hard and we won't get a harder game than tomorrow. But we've been training well and the boys are up for the match.'

He nods in agreement before slipping in the next one.

'Now tell me, what is David Beckham really like?'

I should have known. Even though I've answered this one countless times, I struggle.

'Er, he's a very nice lad. He's worked hard and got his rewards. He was fortunate to be at the right club with the right manager too. He's a great crosser of the ball.'

'Do you know Posh Spice and what's she really like? She always looks a bit moody.' As he says 'moody' he raised his eyebrows, opens his eyes as much as possible and closes his lips in a circle. He looks like Pob, the children's cartoon character.

'I don't really know her (I don't know her at all) but I'm told she's quite a nice person in real life.' I hope Vicky appreciates this endorsement, if our paths do ever cross.

My son, one of four people by the HGV, looks baffled.

'Do you think that one day you can be as good as David Beckham?'

I don't, no, but I gamely reply.

'I'll just keep working hard and do my best, that's all I can do.'

'Well, we're all very proud of you. We know you are very busy, but I'm sure you won't mind sticking around to sign a few autographs.'

I nod and flash the falsest of fake smiles which makes my face hurt. I'd rather drink a gallon of petrol than stay too long. I get down from the HGV as *Movin* by Supergrass starts up. The organiser has hidden depths.

Joan introduces herself and asks if I'd like my face painted. She's serious, I think, yet kindly. I decline.

A granny approaches.

'What's your name again?' she asks. 'Can you sign your signature for my grandson Michael? He supports Manchester United.'

I sign the grubby bit of paper. 'To Michael, best wishes, XX'.

I spot another person, a lad about nineteen, weighing up whether to come and talk to me. The prospect of a real-life conversation seems to have unnerved him, but he approaches, leaving the cover of the beer tent for the drizzle by the HGV.

'My mates think you're shit but I don't mind you, you're a decent player,' he says.

'Thanks,' I reply.

'This must be so embarrassing for you,' adds a lady, who has come from nowhere pushing a big buggy. She's a mum in her early thirties and very attractive. A 'milf' in dressing-room parlance. That's 'Mother I'd Like to Fuck' for those who don't know.

'Good luck tomorrow. My husband is going. He's not shut up about it all week. Says it's the biggest game of the season. He's meeting his mates in the pub at eleven rather than twelve. Says they want to get in the right voice. They all sit together behind the goal. Season tickets.'

'Thanks,' I reply, knowing that she's right. 'It will be hard, but we're up for it.' She flashes me a lovely smile, the one you get when you're a Premier League footballer.

'You fancied that mum didn't you, Dad?' says my son in the car after.

'Lovely wasn't she, son?' I say, 'but not as beautiful as Mum.'

The village fayre was amusingly bad, but I've been there and done that a few times. It was hard as a young pro when I had little experience of such things and was too self-conscious. You're so far out of what becomes your comfort zone, the dressing room. At a fayre near where I grew up, mates from home who came along for a piss up told me that I kept saying 'Yer know' and repeating myself. Mum and Dad, who see a lot in my career but say little, came too. They said nothing.

I could do anything and Mum wouldn't pass an opinion. I like the way she doesn't judge me, but if she's not happy about something then she doesn't need to tell me. I just know.

Mum and Dad said nothing a few years ago when they were watching me warm up from the away end and six or seven lads started singing that I was 'a cunt'. That's six or seven who were supporters of my team. I looked at them and they carried on, as if I'd given them encouragement.

That was awful and affected me hugely. It came because I wasn't playing well – precisely the moment I needed support. It's the worst abuse that I've ever had in my career because it was so close, loud and in front of most of the people I respected in the world, my teammates, my parents and the fans. I was only fifteen yards from it, my parents were three or four, not that the fans knew who they were. I didn't want my mum to see or hear that. I went back into the dressing room after the warm up wondering whether I was in the right profession. Really, it was that bad. There's no happy ending with me dramatically proving them wrong either – we lost. My parents didn't mention it and neither did I. They knew I'd deal with it in my own way and I did.

The irony was that I saw the same group of fans at a McDonald's in a service station after the game. And they saw me. Not one of them said a word.

I thought: 'You fucking cowards,' but I didn't say anything. A group of them and me alone – well, alone but for my parents, who'd given me a lift as the match was close to where they lived. The manager was fine with that.

That's all in the past. I think I proved them all wrong and I know I'm popular with fans, but you're only ever five bad games away from a return to such abuse.

You're not a target during public visits because people appreciate you giving your time. I once visited a school wearing a suit – I was young and wanted to make a good impression. I probably did, but when I arrived the teacher asked me to show the kids some skills outside. So I walked onto a muddy piece of grass and was slipping about everywhere keeping the ball up and getting mud on my pants.

At another school, I'd agreed to coach some of the kids. They were eleven and, with it being a rugby-playing school, had never really played football before. It would have been easier training my nan to curl a free-kick over a wall. And I remember fondly a first visit back to my old senior school, where the teachers who hated me because I messed about too much were lining up to tell me how well I'd done. The old school teacher who'd written a letter to the football club which he wrongly claimed led to my first trial was feeling proud in the reflected glory. I did a question-and-answer session for the kids in their assembly while I was there. The first five questions were: 'How much do you earn?', 'How many sports cars do you have?', 'Are you going out with a supermodel?', 'Does your house have a swimming pool?' and 'What is David Beckham really like?'

At least I got the schools correct. When I was twenty-two, I drove to a school to present awards after an invite through a friend of a friend. The school was busy when I arrived early one evening and the headmaster was speaking. I walked into the main assembly hall and sat at the end of the row of teachers. There were parents opposite and pupils in the centre. A sports teacher whom I knew came and said hello and asked how things were. Half an hour later, I asked him when I was doing the presenting.

'I wasn't aware that you were,' he replied. 'I'll just check.' He then told me that nobody seemed to be aware that I was coming to the options evening for the school. I'd only gone to the wrong school. I was so embarrassed and didn't drive to the other school, but straight home. My name was probably mud there. I felt a complete idiot.

Teammates have some funny stories about public engagements. One went to open a new soccer centre and kicked a ball, which ended up hitting a five-year-old on the face, knocking him on the floor and giving him a nosebleed. The child's father, who heard about this in the bar, then came out and wanted to square up to the player. He got out of there sharpish.

Another player became so friendly with the single mother of one young boy after one awards ceremony that he accepted her invitation to go to hers a week later when her son was staying at his dad's. He slept with her.

THE SECRET PLAYER

I wasn't involved in one of the most humiliating public appearances. At a former club, the new kit was launched in a nightclub, with three models wearing the away kit and three players the home kit. All were to walk down a flight of stairs wearing the full rig, the players wearing their boots too. Nobody had thought through how lethal the combination of metal studs and glass stairs would be. One player slipped, landed awkwardly on his wrist and heavily sprained it.

FA Cup 5th round day against table-topping opponents and there are more people around the ground at 11a.m. when I arrive than usual, more home and more away fans. The visitors received 4,500 tickets and sold them all. The game is a sell-out and I've been pestered for tickets all week. Everyone wants to go to see the best team in the country and it feels like everyone wants to see us beat them. You get comments wherever you go, good luck wishes in the petrol station or supermarket. They're proud people and they'll be right behind us especially if we play well. I'm buzzing for the match, a feeling of excitement and anticipation which I'll miss when I stop playing. There's a crowd outside the main entrance, they're waiting for the visiting team to arrive but they're more vocal with us when we arrive too. They applaud us as we get off the bus and you can hear the shouts of 'Come on!' They're up for it, so are we. We're only two games from a Wembley semi-final, our bonuses have been increased and we'll get another £20,000 a man if we win today.

Money and success are entwined. There were ticket touts at our training ground earlier in the week offering money for tickets for the Cup match. Some of the young pros sold their allocation and probably doubled their weekly wage. I don't think footballers should be touting tickets, but plenty do and the managers are often complicit in turning a blind eye or taking a cut of the pool themselves.

During the warm up I see the TV studio with the country's main analysts in there. As I go back into the stand I'm told that the pundits have been talking about my role and how I can be a key man. That gives me a lift, boosts my confidence, my ego.

The match goes by so quickly. We have a lot of possession, we have chances, we play as well as we have all season. And we lose 1–0. Their striker, who earns £90,000 a week, did almost nothing, but when he had a half chance he took it. Goal. That's why he earns three times more than most of us. One tiny bit of skill, an extra bit of quality which none of our boys have and we're out of the Cup. The striker isn't even fast, but he uses his body and excellent first touch to create half a yard on his marker and make some space for himself. Sheer class and we know it. They're good enough to hold on to that lead.

I'm gutted but half expected it. Football lends itself to disappointment and this is just another of those days in football's pecking order. We were the beneficiaries in the last round. We had more quality than the Championship side, while the best team in the country had more quality than us. I think 'if only' but I won't dwell on the defeat and nor will our manager who tells us that we can be proud, that we've let nobody down and that we must now concentrate on the league which was always our priority.

I pass through the mixed zone. A couple of journalists want

to speak to us, but the rest are waiting for the big stars. I watch our opponents, they radiate a powerful, almost touchable aura. They actually look better than we do because of this halo effect, their skin seems clearer, their haircuts superior, their posture straighter. This is what is meant by star quality.

And some of our fans, who'd booed the away team for ninety minutes and tried to make life as uncomfortable as possible for them, are now waiting for their autographs before they board their team bus, which is also better than ours. We'd appreciate a trip to Wembley or a Cup win far more than them because it would all be new to us, but tough shit, life's not fair and they'll have their own pressures. They need to win every week to keep criticism at bay, we need to stay out of the relegation zone.

We're out of the Cup, which has become our focus for a couple of weeks. We're also only eight points clear of the relegation zone. That's the reality, but at least I'm playing well and injury free in February.

I couldn't say the same a few years ago. I wasn't playing well and the new manager didn't like me. I was one of his top earners and I suspect that he wanted me off the wage bill. He couldn't sell me as the January window had passed, so he suggested that I went on loan in a bid to get me more football and, as I wasn't playing as much as I liked, I agreed. The team I went on loan to was doing very well. They needed me to replace one of their best players, who was injured. It could have all gone so well, yet it was the worst ninety-two days (the maximum for a domestic loan period) of my career.

I was living in a hotel away from my family, who, in turn, were away from our support network of our parents. I felt like an outsider at the new club because I was an outsider. The other players were friendly enough, but they weren't going to invest time into becoming best mates when I was riding off into the sunset in three months.

I wouldn't be surprised if they resented the money I was on too – even though their club were only paying 30% of my wages.

Worst of all, I was useless. I went on loan because I wasn't in shape. If I'd been a world beater every week I wouldn't have been sent on loan, so my confidence and fitness were nowhere near 100%. Replacing a very good player didn't make it any easier for me either, nor did being perceived to be a better player from a higher league. Opponents wanted to prove a point to the 'big timer' even though I'm not big time. They'd make comments during matches such as: 'Been fucked off and sent here because you're shit?' and try that little bit harder to prove the point. They were right – that's exactly how I felt.

I couldn't wait for the loan period to finish and get back, have a rest and start again pre-season. I have mixed feelings about loan moves because of my own experience, but I try to be balanced when young professionals come and ask me for advice about going out on loan themselves.

Loan periods can work. There are lads on the first few rungs of their career here who've gone out to Championship and League One clubs and really benefited. Reserve-team football does not provide an adequate stepping stone for the Under-21s. It's been reduced to infrequent matches between nineteen-year-olds in front of a couple of hundred people at a local non-league ground. It doesn't work, nor does it prepare the player for the reality of competitive football.

The first thing a young player finds when they go on loan is that they're up against an ageing pro who doesn't just want his win bonus, but needs his win bonus. He'll know the tricks, the little digs when the ref isn't looking, the shirt-pulling when needed and the aggressive tackling. This provides far more of an education than any reserve football. I learned far more in my first few months in the first team than all my time in the stiffs.

I'm in favour of copying the Spanish model, where reserve teams play up to the second division and talented youngsters get a dose of what it's really like. They have to learn to speak to the media, to deal with irate fans and horny groupies, to go to famous stadiums where there are thousands of fans and get changed in dressing rooms which don't have jacuzzis. Far better to learn this way rather than coming up against an uninterested pro who has been dropped and told to play in the reserves. I've been that pro and no matter how hard I tried, you lose your competitive edge and relax subconsciously when you know that so little is at stake in the game.

My agent calls one day after training. He's OK and has always negotiated me better deals than I expected. I sort of trust him, but I don't dare to think how much he's made from me over the years and I don't doubt that he will disappear from view when I stop making him money.

He tells me that it's time to start talking about a new contract. Clubs don't like you to get as far as the last year of your deal because you can hold out and leave for free at the end of your contract. I've got sixteen months left and my agent tells me that he's confident that I can get a new deal on similar terms to what I'm on. That will be a first because ever since I've started my wages have gone up and up. The agent tells me to be smart and assertive around the club, to work hard and be seen by the chairman, to sign autographs and make myself available for any public engagements so that I can be viewed of more of an asset to the club.

I can see where he's coming from, but his call has come when I've hit a bad patch, the inconsistency which has stymied me throughout my career. My touch has deserted me and, just as I have no idea why it has done that, I have no idea how to recover my lost form. Experience teaches you that you can only wait until everything mysteriously clicks back into place.

Meanwhile, I continue to embarrass myself by making a hash of things which I could normally do in my sleep. Take yesterday's away game against a team below us in the League. Our winger beat his man and ran towards the by-line. I knew where he'd send the cross and drifted back to meet it. The ball was perfect and I swivelled to connect with it on the volley.

I missed. The ball hit my standing foot before the centre half cleared it.

Thousands of fans in the home end roared with laughter. I was cursing to myself, thinking, 'What happened there? I should have buried that.'

I looked to the bench. Heads were down, no eye contact. A twenty-year-old teammate with five first-team appearances told me to get on my game.

I got slaughtered after the match. By fans, journalists and former professionals. The latter hurt most. I know they are paid to give their opinions and they can't just say nice things and talk in clichés, but it still seems like they are turncoats. There's a code of honour among footballers never to speak ill of each other in public. It's just the way it is, you learn it because you never hear any player saying negative things. What's the point? It's only going to cause ill feeling and problems.

Critical former pros are hated by footballers. There's one who gets paid to spout off about our club. He's the self-styled club legend who never had a bad game back in the day when everything was perfect, unlike today when everything is wrong. His life is a mess, yet he puts himself across as the guardian of football's standards.

He should know better than to speak like a pub bore publicly, should know that there are always issues behind the scenes at a football club where not everything is always as it seems. He just seems bitter that he finished football as a big-name player but with very little financially to show for his efforts. I'm told he was a great player, but he's soiled his image with the current squad because they see his digs as personal. To his readers, he's 'telling it like it is'.

We saw him coming out of a ground recently after we'd won and were getting back on the team coach. A player opened the skylight and shouted: 'Write about that, you twat.' He ignored us, nothing that he hasn't heard before, obviously. When the former player got into a spot of bother and his ill-fortune made the papers, we loved it and pinned it up on the dressing-room door.

Maybe I'm taking what he said too personally because it's closer to the truth than I'd like to admit.

Agents always go for the most optimistic scenario. If they

can't talk up their client who can? It's not like I can send my mum to see the chairman is it? Agents always try and get what's absolutely best for their client because that's usually what's absolutely best for them.

I have to put contract ideas to the back of my mind and crack on with the reality of being a footballer. Of training, games, resting, injuries and a drug test. You get drug tested frequently. I know there are 'revelations' in the press about players going years without being tested – but that's because it's a lottery. I've gone a season when I haven't had a single drug test – and I've had seasons where I've been drug tested six or seven times. There's no pattern, except the drug testers turn up at the training ground or at the club after a game and the club secretary will come into the changing room and say 'the following four players have been picked out by drug testers'. You are then led away into the canteen, where there's a stack of water bottles waiting for you. You drink water until you are ready to provide your sample by urinating into a bottle while someone watches you from behind. You sign a sheet to confirm that the sample was yours and go home.

I know one full professional lad who tested positive. I'm not even going to say what for because it was so rare that it would be easy to work out. He received sympathy and help, not that he learned from his mistakes. You don't last five minutes in top-level football if you're a regular drug user.

I've known a few apprentices fail tests for cannabis. They get a second chance. Weed can stay in your system for a long time and they may have claimed that they took it before they signed their contracts. That should serve as a serious warning.

There are more serious allegations of blood doping. I've

never come across any, but had a former teammate who insisted on seeing his own doctor back in Europe rather than the club doctor. I could never work out why.

Football isn't an endurance sport which lends itself to doping like rugby or cycling. You don't pass the ball better if you're on something – at least I don't think that you do.

Before our final game of February, a teammate who I'm close to approaches me with an interesting proposition regarding money. No, it's not a message from his financial advisor to meet me only 'for a coffee'. Which, if I go, will involve a man in a cheap suit trying to sell me off-plan property in Bulgaria. Or maybe the country has changed and it's now South Africa. A few lads I started out with made it and put money in Bulgarian ski resorts on the promise of future riches which never materialised. Others bought 'off plan' in Morocco on the promise that England internationals and famous actors would be in the same gated community. The artist's impressions made it look like a dream world. Don't they always? Except the development was never built and those footballers' money is still in limbo.

Plenty have bought in Spain, Portugal and the Caribbean, for their own use as well as an investment. If they bought before the economic crash then they've done well, if they didn't then they haven't and they are nursing losses. Others have bought after the crash, hoping to cash in on rock-bottom prices.

I've put my own money into property around the UK. I must have a dozen places now and a couple abroad. In the UK they're sensible three-bedroom family homes in desirable areas of towns and cities. The ones at home are all let through a management company who take their 4% off the rent. And I've got my own financial advisor whom I do trust. I knew him before I made it as a footballer and I like the fact he says 'no' if I ever go to him with some of the schemes with which I'm approached.

The teammate has an idea. We both know that only one of us is going to start the match and we genuinely don't know who. I've played three of the four games so far in February, he's played two and we play in a very similar position. The manager has said that one of us will start the next match.

'Why don't we split the appearance money?' suggests the teammate a day before the match. 'Whoever starts should say that he has a tight calf with fifteen to go. Then you or I go on and we get the appearance money.'

You get appearance money the moment you step on the pitch. It's £6,000 per game in our case. I agree to his plan. We're tight and nobody else needs to know. It's win/win for us – it will just cost the club another £6,000.

After sixty-seven minutes I see my number being held up on a board. I'm brought off and replaced by my teammate. We didn't need to do our plan, but we were both up for it. He wants to go into management himself, so I bet he'll be suspicious of any player who has a tight calf late in a game.

Some managers will say that there are injuries which are all in the mind and invented by players as an excuse because they don't want to play. I've been honest, but there are one or two 'sick note' players at every club I've been at where I've been doubtful about whether their injury is physical or mental. You can't point the finger because you have no evidence, but I've also seen players being asked to play when they're injured by desperate managers. Players take too many cortisone injections and end up doing themselves longer term damage in their knees or ankles.

I've also played when I shouldn't have, because I wasn't strong enough to stand up to the manager and tell him that I wasn't fit. I needed a hernia operation when I was twenty-two. Within ten days I was under pressure from the manager to go back and play. The physio was weak, easily intimidated and sided with the manager – his boss. The manager's job was at stake and so was the physio's. My long-term health came a poor second to their short-term futures. I played, risking a breakdown and even more surgery. I could have been out of the game for a year and know lads whose hernias have given them serious problems, but I got away with it. I was stupid and should have put myself first and taken independent medical advice.

I learned all this the hard way. Another time, I let the club doctor inject cortisone into my knee through a needle so that I could play a game. It's a cold feeling, like someone putting ice in your veins, and it numbs the pain. In my case, the pain was coming from inflammation around a strain in my knee. I should have rested it, not played on it and risked a far more serious injury like damaging my ligaments.

Instead, I became wrapped up in a load of macho bullshit, flattered by the manager calling me 'brave as a lion', praising my spirit and saying that I was the type of player he loved because I had a great attitude and put the team first. It was all self-serving. I should not have played and would not play in similar circumstances now. But I was young; I was an idiot who didn't know better. Thankfully, I got away without picking up a further injury once again, though my knee was twice as sore once the painkiller wore off.

Every pro will tell you stories of the pressure they've been under to play while injured. I didn't rest long enough after one hamstring injury and was rushed back after six weeks. Suspicious, I went to see an independent specialist. She just shook her head and said that the injury was so severe that I should have been out for at least twice that.

There are a lot of angry former footballers with knackered knees who feel very, very bitter at the damage that was done to them by playing while injured because they were put under pressure to do so. There are others who received shoddy operations which curtailed their careers – and their livelihoods. They despise football now, though I think they appreciate that the PFA will help out and pay the cost of private operations. They're good like that.

I often wonder why the media obsesses over nonsense issues like mind games when there are very real issues affecting former players, but then the papers are all about now and washed-up old players don't make headlines.

So we get to read stories about 'mind games' around this time of the year. Ask most footballers what they think of 'mind games' and they'll laugh it off as something that the media and supposedly Alex Ferguson are obsessed with. I spoke to a manager before writing this (and before Fergie stepped down) and he said: 'Fergie is the only one who can afford to play mind games. Try doing it in the Championship and it would quickly bite you on the arse.' There's no kidding anyone with smoke and mirrors the lower you go. Yet to say they don't exist is a lie. I've seen countless psychological acts which don't make the media, yet they have the same intention and potential effect – that of hoping to upset or unsettle an opponent.

One top-flight player did try the media route a few years ago. He claimed in the tabloids that the hard man from a team they were about to play wouldn't have lasted five minutes in the non-league teams where he'd started out. There was only one problem, that wasn't true because he was a genuine tough nut.

Match day came and the hard man got to the away ground, changed down to his underwear and then, rather bizarrely, made himself a cup of tea. Then he calmly walked out of the dressing room.

'Where you going?' asked his manager.

'Don't worry, back in five minutes,' he replied.

He then walked into the home team dressing room and, cup of tea in hand, said to the player who had been questioning his reputation: 'Played with harder players than me have you? We'll see about that.'

The home team were spooked by his serenity and confidence, the mouthy player especially so. The visiting hard man had established himself as the top dog by doing nothing more than stripping to his boxer shorts and making himself a brew. He was later on the winning side and he didn't have to put himself about.

Another up-and-coming manager was big on sports psychology. I was an away player at his club and saw that he'd ordered the placing of big pictures of his team's greatest moments all around the visiting dressing room. They were aggressive, triumphalist pictures of them scoring. The message was clear: watch out, you're next. In the tunnel before the game, his players were high-fiving each other and saying things like: 'Work time!' 'Let's go!' and 'Who wants it?'

Hand on heart, I was quite impressed at how pumped up they appeared. I'm a big lad, but I found them quite intimidating. They seemed so united, until one of our players, a hot-headed little winger, shouted at one of their biggest lads: 'Oi, X, is your mum still shagging all them drug dealers on the estates in London?' The mood changed instantly. The other player was furious and went for him – insulting someone's mum usually does the trick. Our player had thrown a spanner into their heads which no sports psychologist was expecting.

We won 2–0 and they weren't high-fiving each other in the tunnel after the match.

The up-and-coming managers are often the ones who try to make a name for themselves by being different – or 'revolutionary' as their fans have it if they win. At one pre-season friendly, a Premier League team went to a fourth division side who were managed by someone who became very well known. It was a good gesture by the top-flight team and the gate was decent, so why did the young manager of the home team stand on the side bellowing: 'Get stuck in, break his legs.' He was trying to intimidate the visiting players – or 'big-time fucking superstars' as he referred to them, but it was a friendly. Granted, such comments were the norm when I started playing, but not in friendlies.

The more experienced manager calmly walked over and announced: 'If I hear that again then I'm taking my players off the field.' The upstart had no choice but to shut up – it was the home fans who would have been complaining because they would have paid good money for next to nothing.

Another manager, whose star shone very brightly for a season or two, created an 'us against the world' siege mentality. His sides played a terrible long-ball game, but they got results for a while. He was aggressive to the point of having a go at one of his players who'd shaken hands with the other team too enthusiastically after one game. The player, a decent pro, was flabbergasted. Eventually, the manager lost the respect of his players, and, like the others I've mentioned, his 'mind games' showed him up as a one-trick pony.

And who can forget Glenn Hoddle, who tried to get his players to see the faith healer Eileen Drewery? Ray Parlour reluctantly went to see her and she put her hands on his head. 'Short back and sides please, love,' he grinned. There was no way she was getting into his mind.

March

Professional footballers have to vote for their players of the year at the start of March. Everyone in the Professional Footballers' Association gets a vote, but it's baffling why we don't vote at the end of the season, but are balloted when there are nearly three months of it left.

I'm told the reason used to be that the votes took a long time to gather and process, but technology now exists for it to be done in minutes.

The club captain or PFA rep (often the same person) will receive the voting forms and hand them around the dressing room. He'll explain how they need to be filled in and at our club the captain makes them as idiot-proof as possible. Yet players still get them wrong.

There's a lad in our dressing room who is a touch gullible. We always set him up and wait for him to take the bait. We were watching the F1 warm up lap and someone a bit smarter piped up that he was impressed that a 'normal Mercedes was leading against all the real racing cars'.

'That's the practice car,' Gullible corrected him, like we didn't know – to howls of derision. We've set him traps ever since.

'Who are the two teams in the Old Firm match?' asked a player in the canteen last week, 'Rangers and ?' The other lads were in on it and were saying, 'Don't know' or 'Is it Aberdeen?'

'Rangers!' blurted out Gullible to more cheers.

Or when we found ourselves watching a rugby game on television in a hotel. Most footballers have limited interest in rugby, but it was a top match.

'Have you seen how high that player jumps in the line-out?' asked a mischievous player.

'He's not jumping that high by himself, he's getting help from others,' replied Gullible.

Wahay!

He's a good lad, just a bit daft, and there's no way that he's going to be able to fill out an A3 form which has been folded in two. Each player must write in their player of the year, their young player of the year and also their best XI from that season from the division which they play in.

Gullible really struggled with the spelling of 'Ferdinand', so he gave up and voted for 'Terry' instead. No Polish player will ever get a vote from Gullible, he struggles even to make a stab at his name.

The votes are not always an accurate reflection. I'm a fan of one club, so I'm not going to vote for players from our rival teams. Petty? Yes.

A lot of footballers will have a preference for one big club.

Because they're footballers, they've never really been proper fans. When their mates started going to home games at fourteen, they were playing every Saturday; when those mates started going to away games at seventeen, they were young professionals. That's how it was for me and the vast majority.

Because you're playing, you can't support your local team in the truest sense, so you end up siding with a team who are always on television because you are away so much and turn to the TV to break the boredom.

There are many latent fans of the big six who've played against them more often than they've paid to see them play. And, if you're a Liverpool fan but playing for Aston Villa, you are not going to be as inclined to vote for Manchester United or Everton players.

Personal grievances come into the voting too. Lads don't vote for people they don't like and reasons for disliking someone are numerous. They may not like his image; they may have heard bad things about him; they may know him and dislike him. Or, they may have been outclassed or kicked by a player.

Other players don't take the voting seriously. I've seen two Reading players put in the central midfield of the Premier League team of the year; seen one lad disappear into the toilet cubicle and wipe his arse with the voting form because he suspected that none of us would be in the team of the year.

The PFA are not stupid. If the players at a club don't fill the forms in properly, then no players from their club can be included in any of the awards, which are given out at an awards dinner in a five-star London hotel one Sunday night at the end of April. The captain usually gets the votes in at the last minute, but it would probably be easier for him to herd up cats. I guess I can see why the PFA need to allow so long to gather the votes.

We have more important issues to think about than PFA voting. Freshness is the name of the game now as we come towards the end of the season and the intensity of vital games coming in quick succession. There would be even more games if we hadn't been knocked out of both domestic cup competitions and if we were playing in Europe like some of the biggest teams. They have the squads to compete for trophies on three or four fronts, we don't. Our greatest asset is that we're in the Premier League, and staying there is our priority.

The manager comes into his own in March. Or he should do. He needs to select the right teams with the freshest players. The secret is not necessarily putting out your best team, but picking the freshest. We have several international players and they're not fresh when they come back from representing their various countries, especially if they involve a long flight. Unlike at the top clubs, there are no private jets back from Argentina at our club so that they can get back smoothly and quickly.

Tiredness is a great leveller – but we use that to our advantage against teams packed with global stars. We need to pick up points. We're 14th, but just six points above 18th.

It's easy for me to talk about freshness and throw in some cod psychology. The reality is that there are issues in the dressing room, specifically with one player, who is not in the manager's future plans. Another club made a solid bid for the player in January and our club agreed to sell him. Readily. He's one of our best earners and he's on the bench more often than not.

The club want him off the wage bill. There are rumours that some large-scale team rebuilding might be happening in the close season. The offer was from another Premier League club, but on less money than he's currently paid – and a four-hour drive from where he lives. He turned it down, as he was entitled to. That infuriated the manager and the chairman. The manager has been on his case ever since, making sure that he's in every single day for training and that he's never a minute late. In fact he's been on his case since he started nudging him out of the team in the autumn. The manager had made a footballing decision, nothing more. He wasn't as influential in games as the gaffer hoped. The player drives in every day, a three- to four-hour return journey. If he's a few seconds late, he's fined.

Other players are shown far greater leniency, but a point is being made here. Problem is, the player is never late. It has become personal. He knows he'll be fined an eye-watering 20% of his wages. On Christmas Day, none of us thought we'd see him. Our session was a short one, he wasn't named in the squad for Boxing Day. He would have to drive all that way for a one-hour light session, leaving his family on Christmas Day. We thought he'd take a hit.

Instead, he realised that he could fly by helicopter for £4,000 – a lot less than any fine would be. The helicopter flight would be twenty-five minutes each way. When a helicopter landed on the training ground and the player got out, the manager was fuming. But what could he do? 'Landing on the training ground in a helicopter' was not on the list of misdemeanours which attract fines, alongside such crimes as being late, using your mobile phone in the canteen or leaving training gear on the pitch.

Last month, after the player turned down the January move, the manager told him that he was going to be training with the first-year professionals – the seventeen-year-old lads. He is a hard-faced bastard and he did it, but the manager hoped that the player would break and move in the summer, rather than sit out the remaining year on his very good contract. Once again, the player responded. The youth team coach apologised to the player ahead of the first training session, explaining that it wasn't ideal that he was there, but that the manager was the boss and what he said went. The player was calm the about whole thing. He knows the score and enough people in the game to ask advice. And one of them advised him to go in hard on the young lads, which is exactly what he did. Within twenty minutes of the first training session, the youth team coach had pulled him off the field for being far too aggressive.

'It's my natural game,' replied the player, when the youth team coach expressed his fears that his young charges would be seriously injured. The player, who consulted the PFA at every turn, returned to training with the first team. The PFA didn't advise him to be aggressive, but they did advise him of his rights.

None of this helps the mood. We're not one-for-all and all-for-one and our form has suffered. José Mourinho thinks that 'success is down to players, failure down to the manager'. By saying that he's covering himself (not for the first time), but while he has a point, no player wants to be relegated.

Your wages are cut in half for a start, your bonuses dry up and it doesn't look good on your CV. I've been in a team that has been relegated before and everything about it was awful.

We were getting abuse from our own fans who knew that we were going down. The manager became more tense and emotional because he realised that he was going to lose his job. Individually, other managers stop looking at you because you're in a losing side – you're officially a loser. You lose the cachet of being a Premier League footballer, something that less than 500 people can boast. You lose confidence, in your own ability, your manager and your teammates. Everything is negative and losing becomes a habit. It's like being in a whirlpool. Nobody wants to be there, but you start to go down and down.

People try to arrest the slide. The chairman will start showing up at the training ground a lot more. The fans will be on his case too and you can bet that he'll let the manager go if the pressure gets too much on him.

There are other symptoms of a side in a slide towards relegation. Players go missing in games, they don't shout for balls as they did because they know that mistakes are more likely. They hide and keep their heads down because they're feeling the pressure, the negativity and the criticism all around them. Some players don't even make it to the pitch and seek respite in the treatment room. They're losing out on a stack of appearance money, but some players just can't hack the pressure, no matter how good they are as footballers.

Their calf strain, which should take two weeks to recover takes four weeks. A calf or hamstring strain is one injury which can be open to interpretation. The physio will ask the player how it feels. The player can stretch the truth for his own benefit.

The very biggest clubs are installing hugely expensive machines in their training grounds which can identify soft tissue injuries before they occur. They can also scan for a more accurate prognosis than the one given by the player. Thus the scope for embellishment is reduced. You can't get away with anything on the pitch now because of the cameras. And you can't get away with anything off it because of cameras – everyone has a camera in their phone and the scanners can look inside your body. Honesty really will be the best policy for a footballer from now on.

When I started out, injuries were treated with ice followed by a heat pad. Now, it's known that adding heat to an inflamed area is the worst thing to do. Players don't take hot baths after matches, because the heat will only inflame all the micro tears in your muscles. We take an ice bath instead – and then a shower rather than a soak.

The biggest clubs are bringing as much of their medical side in-house as possible for a couple of reasons. One, it's more private. How many big-name transfers have been announced with a player turning up for a medical at a private hospital not owned by the club? If the player fails that medical, it's in the interests of the player and both clubs for that not to be public. Also, it's better to keep everything in-house. New machines give players heart screenings to detect any unforeseen problems too. It's all progress and I'm not adverse to the advancements. You simply can't turn off and pretend that there are not improvements.

When I began my career, players did bench presses in the gym. Knowing what I know now, it was ridiculous. Bench presses make you better at pushing people in a forward motion, which one or two footballers may find useful. They don't help your physique as a footballer.

In the past, players would hit the gym and lift as much as they could. There was a lot of bravado involved, but when you're a player, elements like balance and stability are more important than being a beefcake. Some players do need to hit the weights to beef up, but you don't need big arms because you don't really use them in football. When you do weights, it's far more targeted, usually following the results of time strapped up in an Isokinetic machine. This registers the strength and weakness in various parts of your body. At the start of this season, I discovered what I'd always known, that my left leg was considerably weaker than my right. I was given exercises to build up my left side.

Now, training is more about replicating real match scenarios, so there are few long-distance runs in straight lines because games aren't like that. There will be more work done on speed and stamina, so that players can get an edge over the first three or four yards. The need for speed is paramount and players are always trying to help themselves become quicker.

A former teammate had his bedroom done out with an £8,000 oxygen altitude tent. Professional cyclists and some athletes swear by this, claiming it stimulates the body to work at a higher altitude, where there is less oxygen (12% in a tent rather than 21% outside at sea level). Red blood cells are stimulated to carry oxygen to the body and your muscles get more oxygen. More oxygen makes it easier to run more. He believes he can feel the benefit, though I don't suspect that Paul Scholes has one at home.

One area of advancement which I'm not convinced about

is football boots and the way they are continually marketed as being better because they are lighter. To the impressionable or young mind, the implication is that if you buy the same boots as Lionel Messi then you can play just like him. All absolute nonsense; marketing and style triumphing over substance. Nobody is saying that wearing the heavy, stiff leather boots which players wore in the 1930s is going to make it any easier to play football, but in a huge, lucrative industry dominated by Nike and adidas, the hype has gone too far.

I've always liked black adidas Copa Mundials made from kangaroo leather (not that adidas advertise that they are made from dead marsupials). They are simple, black, light-weight, comfortable and reasonably hard-wearing. I go through about ten pairs a season. Puma Kings are similar; classic football boots which are decent in summer and winter – as are the Nike Tiempos. They all come with either moulded studs or screw-in studs for softer ground. I'm entirely comfort-able with them, but we're constantly pushed towards newer boots. I simply don't like them and see them as a fashion accessory. I sound like a granddad already, but black leather boots have served me fine and I'll continue to wear them.

Nike are clever. They turn up at our training ground pre-season with a cool-looking truck stocking every boot and every size. The young players are all over them, the pink and orange boots and all that nonsense. They really do fill their boots and walk away with several pairs.

My concern with the ultra-light boots is that they offer little protection. They were scrutinised after a spate of high-profile metatarsal injuries to players like Wayne Rooney, but you don't have to break a bone to have a foot injury. I missed one game after injuring myself kicking the bottom of some-body's boot. The bruising was horrendous and that was with 'normal' boots which offered much more protection than the newly fashionable ranges.

Other players (most Premier League) will have a boot deal. For me, it might be worth £50,000 a year. A smaller company like Hi-Tec or Mizuno could afford me and I'd happily wear their boots. They'll have a relationship with a rep of the company and an agreement to be available for an amount of time during the contract. That time will be divided up into doing interviews (where the player is pictured in the boots), but the journalists can ask about general football matters. Duncan Ferguson signed a boot deal, but was reluctant to do the media part. He agreed to one interview but told the journalist that he would only speak about his boots. The interview was a farce, because he refused to answer most of the questions, unless they were related to his boots.

Some players think that the sponsorship money is just extra spending money without strings. They're used to having their tax deducted at source and don't realise that they have to pay income tax on sponsorship deals until they're hit with a big bill.

I usually spend a few hours in on the day before a match – a Friday afternoon. Today, my plans are changed a little. We do a media day on the Friday before a Saturday match. The manager does five sets of interviews. First, he speaks to the local papers, then to the nationals, then to the Sunday papers, then the television and finally radio. It takes him an hour every Friday but he's good at it. He comes across as he is – someone in control with the confidence that comes from being a good manager. Journalists trust him and know they can't take the piss. He's not afraid to pull them up if a story has upset him either. One paper appeared to have it in for a player with a few negative stories – the manager told the journalist that their target's mother had been diagnosed with a serious illness and he could be excused for not being 100%. Such off-the-record briefing helps all concerned.

Two players will help the manager out by giving the media more interviews. The demands have only increased in my time in football, though we're still small fry at our club. I did a ground tour at the Bernabéu and the press conference room was the size of a theatre. Most of the senior players will speak to the media and any of the younger lads who are reasonably articulate. We help them out so that they don't say 'yer know', every ten seconds like I used to do. This week is my shift and a journalist, not unreasonably, asked me how contract negotiations are going. I give a non-committal answer, something about how my agent is going to speak to the chairman. I have to be careful what I say. If I appear too keen to sign then that weakens my bargaining position – that's if they want me.

I've started to be asked about my future on Twitter too. I'm on there, but I have mixed feelings about it and my advice to other players would be not to bother because the cons outweigh the pros. There are players who like it and say it puts them in direct contact with fans, and players are always accused of not being in touch with fans. We'd happily be in touch with fans within limits, but we have to be guarded for the reasons I've outlined.

Players can correct media stories though, put their side of the story across or put people straight if they are misquoted or whatever. Even that is risky. One fan with 8,000 followers was putting it about on Twitter that one of our players wasn't being treated fairly. Truth was, the player had asked for a transfer and that was why he wasn't central to the manager's thinking. A teammate sent the fan a direct message, explaining what was really happening and that the player had asked for a transfer. The fan then leaked this onto social media. The player regretted his intervention.

The Twitter thing is more about ego, with players keen to boost the number of their followers. I did actually get some stick recently off a player for not having as many followers as him and I'm not entirely convinced that he was joking.

I'm on there because someone set up a bogus account in my name and pretended to be me. It was only going a week, but apparently picked up a few thousand followers. He was spilling dressing-room 'secrets' and talking nonsense, though one close mate texted me and said: 'Good luck with your scan.' The false Twitter-me told people that he was having a scan and feared a serious injury.

I informed the press officer and she sorted it by faxing a copy of my passport (the club keeps them on file for trips) to Twitter, who removed the false one and set me up with a real account.

Some players go on there under a bogus name and have ten followers – their close mates who know it's them. I use my identity, but I'm not comfortable on Twitter and I never tweet after we've lost a game when emotions are running high. I don't even look on there at times like that. As well as the abuse (and praise), you get loads of requests for signed shirts. I've been tempted to reply to a few of the critics, but always held myself back because I could see myself saying something which I'd later regret.

The relationship between journalists and footballers is based on equal measures of trust and mistrust. To show off to some friends in a pub, I asked them to name a player who they'd like to see at the club I was at. A realistic name came forward, a Premier League striker who would have really excited fans. In front of their eyes, I called a journalist I knew and told him that I'd heard a bid was imminent. It was the back-page headline on the local paper the next day, with television following it up. All from a one-off phone call. The journalist put too much trust in his source. Me. I couldn't do that every week, but given that every other piece of information I'd given him (which wasn't much) had been accurate, and given my status as a first-team player, they ran with it. The story soon fizzled out with all the other pre-season transfer crap you get and no damage was done.

One manager told me that you have to keep the media onside if you want to survive. Look at how bad it can become when you don't do that when players brief against very good coaches, leaking stuff all over the shop and undermining the team.

I've seen it all before. A key player at one club had his eyes on being the manager. He therefore undermined the manager – a hugely well-known figure – by leaking information to a local journalist about the players not being happy and such like. So the paper had all the inside news on team selection, everything. The club initially tried to deny the leaks, but they started to look stupid because it was all true. Nobody could work out how the paper seemed to know everything that was going on at the club, but they started to suspect when said paper puffed up the chances of the player becoming manager. Which he did. What goes around comes around; it may happen to him one day and I don't think he'll like it.

And yet against all that, the golden rule as a player is to take in as little media as possible. It plays with your head if you start reading the papers – the praise and criticism – you're better without it. Then again, you get to find out what people are saying about you, but it's better if you don't go looking for it yourself.

I was having a hard time at one club and fans were calling for another player to be given a chance. A paper did a feature on that very topic and the player brought the paper into the pre-match meal and put it on the table so we could all see it. I thought he was a prick for doing that, but didn't blame the journalist.

The media have certain topics they'll return to over and over again. Like why there aren't many, if any, openly gay footballers in the British game. I've never played with a player who was openly gay, nor have I suspected any teammate of being gay. The dressing room is a hypermasculine environment, where the talk is of girls and not men.

It would be very, very hard for a player if he came out and continued to play.

I wouldn't have a problem with it and I believe, granted without any evidence, that most footballers wouldn't. The prospect of a gay lad in the dressing room doesn't trouble me in the slightest. There would be a bit of banter, of course, requests to 'stop looking at my cock', but if the gay player was a good lad then there would be no more than that. Being a 'good lad' is more important than skin colour, sexuality or nationality.

The problems for an openly gay player would come from fans. They already joke that some players are gay when they're not – but since when have the facts got in the way of what fans sing?

It would take a brave player to come out and carry on playing, to ignore the wolf whistles and much, much more. If his personality was strong enough, he could ridicule any homophobia from the terraces and show the bigots up for the embarrassment that they are.

But you know what, football might just surprise you. It has a habit of bringing the best – and the worst – out of humans. Look at the reaction when someone dies or is ill. Fans can be great and they might just respect a player who was brave enough to come out.

Match fixing is another issue which the media are desperate to expose. I can honestly say that I've never been offered money to throw a match. Why would I? Apart from it being wrong, it's not like I need the money is it?

I had a call from a former teammate about a League Two match between Accrington and Bury in 2008. So did other players, so something serious must have been going on and it led to several players being suspended. These were lower league lads placing bets of a grand or two and even then suspicious betting patterns were noticed by bookmakers, who called the police. Is it really worth it for a millionaire to bet a grand? I just can't see the point in cheating.

Talk in the dressing room isn't just about relegation. Lads are booking holidays and one big advantage of being knocked out of the FA Cup, of not being in Europe or any potential play-off games, is that we know exactly when our season will finish. We can see the beach. The young guns want to go to Vegas for a lads' holiday, but they know it's going to be tough explaining it to their partners. They know getting a green card will be tough – and they don't mean the green card issued by US immigration, but an imaginary one issued by their Mrs. They're also known as a 'pass out' or a 'pink ticket'. Another player has had to count himself out because he has a criminal record.

The rest hatch a plan. One has asked a young lad in the club office to send an email from a club account, giving details of a one-week end-of-season tour. The office junior protests that he could lose his job, but the first-team player is insistent and the junior relents. He's star-struck and likes the idea of helping out a player. So he sends the following from a club account.

'Dear X,

XX Football Club have confirmed a one-week end-of-season tour to the United States, where we will play two friendly games and participate in two charity days with local hospitals in California.

The trip will be between May 24th and June 1st. Please keep these days free as all first-team members will be required to attend.

We will apply for American visas on your behalf.

Yours,
XXX
Club Office'

The email is then printed out and shown to partners or girlfriends, who, typically, aren't happy because their men will be absent for another week.

One comes in the day after the email is sent and says: 'All done, she's fallen for it.' Another says the same and they high-five each other. Another asks a player if he can pay for the trip as he has a joint bank account and doesn't want his partner to see that he's paid for flights to America. He promises to pay him back in cash.

The lads have put a lot more thought into this than usual, but there are many potential flaws that any wife or girlfriend with a brain will spot.

Firstly, as there are no games because there is no tour, there will be no media reports.

Secondly, the partners talk. A trip to America is bound to crop up in conversation. If every player was going and in agreement then it would be easier to conceal, but only five of them are making the trip. The plan is prey to disaster, though that doesn't stop participants trying to keep their partners apart in the players' lounge after matches so that the subject of Vegas doesn't crop up.

One player even stops his girlfriend going to watch him. He works out there are four home games left and that he can find an excuse for each of them. The first is: 'Let's have an early meal and a big night out on Saturday. Book a table at six. I'll come straight back after the game and meet you at home.' The partner agrees. That's one game out of the way.

Another player, who is not on the trip, drops a bombshell. He tells the players that he's also booked to go to Vegas – with his partner at the end of the season. He's a young pro and he's excited because it's his first year of serious money. There will be no more lads' trips to Ayia Napa as he can now afford to go five star in Vegas. He's surprised at the reaction to his news – the players are furious, but after calming down, they get him to agree to stay away from the hotels where they plan on hanging around.

Inevitably, the girlfriend of one finds out that there is actually no post-season tour to Vegas. She met the wife of a player who is not part of the conspiracy in the supermarket and it didn't take long for the deception to be uncovered. She's not happy, but her man tells her that he's going anyway and that he deserves a break with the lads after a hard season. She can like it or lump it.

They make an agreement that they'll spend the following week at the Burj in Dubai, the hotel often voted the most luxurious in the world.

Luxury holidays are the last thing on my mind when I come out of the stadium after our final game in March, a disappointing 1–1 draw which leaves us just six points clear of the relegation zone with seven games to play. I don't think we'll go down and I'm not complacent enough to be lazy either. We need points.

A fan approaches me as I walk back to my car.

'What the fuck is going on?' he asks, with more desperation and sadness in his voice than aggression. 'We hoped to push for Europe this season, it's all gone tits up.' The fan is a similar age to me, similar build too. He's no clown who can be fobbed off with a one-liner, but he was optimistic in hoping for European football.

I have to be careful what I say because I know it's going to be repeated everywhere.

MARCH

'The lads who are playing are all trying their best,' I say. 'We really are, but it's not easy as you can see. On our day we're good enough, but we're not having our days enough. Or maybe we're not good enough and we'll go down, but I don't think that's the case. What I do know is that we need your support, we really do. We need everyone behind us. We want to stay up.'

The fan listens, nods his head and shakes my hand.

'We'll be right behind you,' he says. I walk off, unexpectedly feeling very moved by his sincerity, a rare moment of mutual understanding across the divide.

April

Bad news. My agent calls and it's no April fool wind up. I'm unlikely to get offered a new contract, which means the club will want to get rid of me in the summer so that they can get money for me. Or, I could just sit on my contract and run it down, but there's no point being around if I'm not part of the manager's plans. And, between the manager, his coaches and the chairman, they've all decided that I'm not. Seems like I should have been more concerned about the replacement than I was. He started well but faded badly when the temperature dropped. Adapting to British football has been a slow process for him and that difficult second season awaits, but they seem to believe he is a better prospect than the devil they know.

My phone rings with the news on the way home from training, after a great session on a beautiful spring morning when I was loving life and football. I was only thinking about how much I liked being at this club. The gaffer didn't even hint at what he knew.

I'm not completely surprised, though. I've sensed that the manager has been trying to palm me off by saying 'We'll get something sorted in the summer.' I know he means well, but his main intention was keeping me happy. I also know that he doesn't have the absolute authority to give me a new contract. He doesn't even know if he'll still be in charge for one, nor what his budget will be for next season if he is. Our usually docile chairman seems to have tired of the annual flirtation with relegation and is agitating for a radical reorganisation of the team, but with no extra cash forthcoming, that means selling some established players.

My agent forced the issue and we've got the answer we were looking for. I'm not stunned by this, it's football. The club did tell my agent that nothing was definite, but it seems definite to me that they want to sell me in the summer. My re-sale value after another contract when I'm thirty-one or thirty-two will be much less.

At least I have the security of another year's contract, something not every player here has. Football retires you; you don't retire from the game. I've heard a lot of older pros say that, the type who tells you to play as long as you can because you're a long time retired. Like every footballer, they looked forward to finishing their career, to being able to do normal things like take a family holiday in August, going out with the family on a Saturday or with their mates on a Friday. But the novelty didn't last long.

Like death and taxes, every pro knows that their career will come to an end; it's just something they don't like to think about. For most, the end is bitter. One player in a thousand will get a fanfare, the luxury of choosing his end at a time to suit in front of adoring fans. For the rest, it's usually a manager saying, 'I'm sorry, I've not got anything for you.'

I've seen it happen to heroes, club legends. He'll go and see the boss, maybe with the slightest of suspicions about what's to come. The boss will thank him for his contribution, weasel some excuse about budgets, say he'll recommend him to others and that's it.

I've seen players walk into a near-empty dressing room, pick up their boots and depart. You don't hang boots up, you take them down. You try to be nice, to shake their hands and wish them well, but they're in a daze with their heads down. The realisation that they are unemployed hits them hard as they drive away from the training ground in a luxury car depreciating at £1,000 a month.

The signs that your days are numbered can't be missed. Away fans calling you fat, not at one club but two. Players over thirty have to work much harder at their fitness. Not rest more, but train more. No alcohol on a Saturday night if you want to stay at the top. You put weight on, it takes longer to come back from injury and you can't get the same times on those shuttle runs. If you're a player who depends on pace, then you're knackered.

As your status drops, you want to try and prove people wrong against a backdrop of shouts like: 'Any chance you can leave us in the summer?' It hurts. It's a private and yet very public ordeal, there's no kidding anyone when you are being judged in front of 35,000 people and scrutinised on television.

The older pros know they can still play and that they've got a lot to give, but they are just not as good as they were. And fans cool on you too, which feels like when a woman turns cold on you and your halo vanishes from above your head. It's not pleasant, but a good manager will know how to use you to your strengths – if you have enough left to justify being picked. If you stop being an automatic starter it becomes even harder. People may pick up on Ryan Giggs or John Terry not being up to pace if they come off the bench, but it's hard to get on the pace of the game at nineteen, let alone thirty-nine.

For many, who are not yet ready to retire, there is always the option of dropping down to a Championship club, another staging post on the road to the end, but a place where they can be one of the best players. Older pros may find they have little say in where they'll go. If an offer comes in for me and the club like it, I'll be put under pressure to sign. The manager might tell me that I'm not in his plans anymore, so I'd face the prospect of reserve football which no pro wants.

And while I'm happy to 'drop down', my agent is eyeing a deal in the Premier League. A journalist close to the club seems to share my agent's optimism. He's told me that the word is that they are considering a new deal for me. I half believe it. He said the same to a former teammate a year ago and he believed it. Then he went to see the manager who trotted out the standard: 'I'm sorry, we've not got anything to offer you.'

One of my best mates was in a difficult situation last year. He was thirty-two and got an inkling that he wouldn't be getting a new contract around November. He was pro-active in what he did and I intend to learn from him. When teams came to play at ours, he deliberately made himself busy before the match, saying hello to opposing coaches and managers in the tunnel around the warm up and coming across as a decent lad. Managers are paranoid about buying the wrong type of player. Joey Barton would have no trouble getting a good club if he was perceived to be a decent lad. Instead, he's viewed as a loose cannon and managers will be cautious with him and probably steer clear. The same could have been said of Eric Cantona, though. Sometimes it just takes the right coach to get the best out of a player, to really understand how he ticks. That's what the great coaches do.

When he met opposing coaches, my mate would shake their hands and ask them how things were, planting a little seed in their mind that he's 'alright'. Managers like good eggs in the dressing room, people who are not going to give them further stress.

He went to the PFA annual dinner in London at the end of April knowing that several managers would be there and spoke to a few, though he didn't push anything. It was the same theory as meeting them at the ground, a chance to creep onto their radar.

I'm intending to do exactly the same, even though it didn't work for him. Another player I know was in demand after finishing a season strongly. It's always better to finish strongly rather than fade because that's when most assessments are made. He was earning good money at a Premier League club, but was offered even better money at another club closer to home in Manchester. He didn't give them an answer because he thought there would be more offers. There were none. When he told them he'd like to join them, the club – Bolton Wanderers – had bought a replacement and no longer wanted him. The player started to flap and was a bit embarrassed as he didn't have a club. He ended up going on trial at a Championship club, where he earned a contract worth a quarter of what Bolton had offered. Timing is crucial in football, on and off the pitch.

Trialists are another part of football about which very little is known to outsiders. Clubs don't publicise when they have a trialist, it's better that way for both parties in case it doesn't work out. And it usually doesn't work out.

Most of the trialists at a Premier League club are young players, mainly foreign. They're treated like second-class citizens by the other players. They wear their own kit or old kit provided by the club. Chances are they're only going to be there a week or two so there's not much point getting to know them. Players have to earn respect to be liked and there's not much chance of a trialist doing that unless he's brilliant. But if he's brilliant, he's hardly likely to be on trial is he?

There are exceptions to what I've said. You'll get experienced, well-known players coming on trial throughout the season. They are afforded the respect their reputations deserve, but it can be sad watching them try and earn a contract at a skint club. I saw one lad who'd been a £10 million player try and fail to win a contract at ours. He ended up dropping down not one, but two, leagues. Lower down the leagues, trials are becoming normal. Contracts are shorter and a mate who played in League One last season said he fully expects to go on trial at the start of next season, where a manager will weigh him up for a week or two. Trials favour the managers as they are afforded a closer look at the players, but the player can only realistically go on two or three trials pre-season before they need a contract. They need to stand a realistic chance of getting a contract and yet there are not enough contracts to go around. So players drop down further.

Managers have a curious, almost paranoid response to trialists. They don't like to take someone else's rejects, though there is a clear pecking order in that respect. There would be no shame in Blackpool taking a player who has been turned down by Man United, for example, but not by Peterborough.

Not all trialists are the real deal. One lad, now a successful agent, came to England to try and make it as a goalkeeper when he was younger. He paid his own way around several clubs and spent a couple of days at each, before being rejected. He started at the top and never gave up, not even when he was chipped by a striker. In a five-a-side goal.

Mr Hopeful went to twelve clubs in total and the best he got was: 'Keep in touch, but we don't have anything for you now.' He was then honest enough to call it a day, but his thick skin and perseverance made him perfect for another line of football work.

So I'm prepared for what might be ahead, but I'm also realistic and reasonably relaxed. You don't go from playing thirty-five games for a Premier League club in one season to playing in the Unibond the next. My agent is totally cool about the situation, advising me not to worry, that there will be plenty of demand for me. There's a nagging voice chipping away inside my head that I could be without a club, but he knows his stuff. We have a couple of months before football stops in June, when nothing happens as everyone disappears on holiday. I once moved between clubs and had to get the two chairmen to speak to each other. One was in Australia, the other Barbados. I fixed it for them to speak for the one time of the day when they would both be awake. Maybe you think an agent should do that, but players should get involved to maximise their chances. But not to do an Odemwingie, driving down to their prospective club, burning bridges and making themselves look too desperate. Maybe the club will accept a deal from another club and get us to agree terms, that's just as likely as transfers come about in several ways.

I've not got an exclusive contract with my agent. That is, he doesn't have a signed mandate to represent me and for nobody else to represent me. He would rather that he did have that, but what if I do a deal myself? What if a former manager calls and makes a verbal offer which I'm happy with? Does my agent really need 5% of that when I've done the deal?

I'm even prepared to ring a few other agents whom I know are close to big-name managers. I won't tell my agent this. If he brings me a deal then the business is his, but if he doesn't I'm open to other options.

So I work the phones, sounding out these other agents. They want the business and, as I am an established Premier League property, they are naturally interested and tell me that they will inform the managers. They also ask what I'm looking for money-wise. I'm getting on as many radars as possible and I see no shame in this, every player in football will be out of contract at some point.

I've also been in the situation before. I know about the

transfer merry-go-round and how it works, with players getting sounded out by coaches and managers. Football's own chain and, like housing chains, such deals are prone to collapse if one move falls through.

One of my projected moves collapsed partly because of my own actions. A few things happened in a short space of time over which I had little control. I was about to sign for a biggish club and was driving there to put pen to paper. Then my phone went off – an emergency call from my agent, who was travelling down in a separate car – ordering me to turn around immediately as my prospective manager was about to be sacked. I'd driven three hours and was within five minutes of the motorway turn-off so I just carried on and drove into the club car park. I don't think anyone spotted me as I pulled up and looked at the club sign outside the main stand. An hour earlier, I had been preparing mentally to represent the team in the sign. My wife was starting to get the idea into her head which would end up with her moving our family 150 miles away. But one dismissal and that was that. I turned around and drove home.

Football can be a shit industry much of the time, but I've been a shit myself. A few weeks later, I made a verbal agreement to join a great old club. Their manager seemed to be going places and I was impressed by him. A medical was arranged, a date set and the word was out among the media close to their club that I was signing.

But then I had a better offer from a club in the same division closer to my house. I would be working for a manager I knew well. I spoke to my wife about it and it was obvious which was the better option for me and our family.

I tried to do the decent thing (and the wise one, given that football is a small world) and rang the boss of the club I had a verbal agreement with to apologise and tell him that I wouldn't be joining his club as I'd had a better offer for me and my family. Which was true.

He went absolutely fucking mad and ranted down the phone for a minute, before telling me that he was going to send the invoice for the medical to my home address (he never did) and finishing off with 'I don't want arseholes like you near my club.'

We played against his team three games into the season and I thought: 'This could be tasty.' But the boss I'd let down merely blanked me. We won 2–1.

I trust my agent. Well, mostly. I'd hate to hear that he's been asking too much money for me, but he assures me that he's not. I know other players who've been priced out of deals because of greedy agents.

Ask any footballer about agents and they're likely to have a less than complimentary story. Agents manipulate players, especially young ones. They groom them. Agents begin by ingratiating themselves with players, stroking their egos, promising to look after them like their own children. Agents are salesmen, often with a good business sense, and footballers are their products.

I can see why they exist, but this unregulated, potentially highly lucrative industry attracts all kinds of sharks. Every agent is supposed to be FA and FIFA registered, but that means little. That's just an exam which anyone with half a brain can pass. And some of the most powerful agents in football are not properly registered. They can't call themselves agents, more 'business advisors', but they are the ones who cut the massive deals.

There are too many agents and not enough of any level of deals to go around. Agents are in it for one thing: themselves. There are some good agents, the ones who have hundreds of contacts, influential contacts. Certain clubs pay agents more than other clubs, so agents favour them and try to propel you towards them, but they are prepared to do you over to keep those clubs sweet.

I had an agent looking after me for a while. I no longer speak to him. He shafted me. He pushed financial advice and products on me that I should never have signed up to, where he cut himself in generously on the commissions.

I strongly suspect – though I can't prove – that he said to one club: 'If I can get him to sign for £15,000 a week, can I get £200,000?' He knew that the club were prepared to pay £20,000 a week for me, but also that I would sign for £15,000. He saved them money and lined his own pockets. It leaves a very bitter taste. I've seen double charging added to that, where an agent concludes a deal and then goes to the player and claims that the club didn't pay him.

A good agent should be an excellent negotiator who is optimistic about his clients. He should have his clients punching above their weight, both in terms of their stature and their wages. He should give hard, no-nonsense advice and keep a player grounded. If he has a player at Sunderland who thinks he's good enough for Arsenal or Tottenham but isn't, then the agent needs to tell him this.

He needs to be like a social worker and speak to his client

when he's playing badly, not just when he's doing well and attracting attention.

He needs to be there for his player, offering emotional support and dealing with a player who wants to know why he's not playing, answering questions about why the manager/fans/teammates don't like him, rather than not picking up his calls.

He should have solid contacts and represent good players. If you're a young player and an agent approaches you and says that he also represents Steven Gerrard, then you'll listen to him. If he has no other players then you'll be less inclined to do so. Agents can build up a portfolio with just one big-name player to attract others – and their big-name player will be the one who keeps their agency going. There's a black agent in London with thirty black players on his books – those lads know they can trust him.

Agents manipulate players but players can also manipulate agents. An agent may approach a player to whom he's not contracted and say that he has a club which is interested in him. They won't be, but the player might raise his eyebrows and feel flattered. But he'll then go to that club and say that the player is interested in joining them.

Some players tell agents to bring offers to them and they'll take it from there before agreeing to sign with them, but agents naturally don't want that.

Despite attempts to sort things out, the system is flawed, with all sorts of chancers trying to cut-in on deals. Clubs use their preferred agents too. One of my former teammates got a big-money move to a top club. He'd used the same agent for years, a reliable fella who negotiated him a decent boot contract and several nice commercial deals. The buying club told him that they only went through a certain agent – who is widely viewed as a crook throughout football. The agent got a call from the crook, saying that he had to cut him in on the deal or there would be no deal. The agent cut him in, there was enough money in the pot for two. Or three, given that the team's manager was almost certainly in on it – that's why the crook got the call in the first place. Everyone wants a piece of the pie.

However, I'm not one of those who believe that players can do without agents. Clubs take the piss without them; they did for decades. They'll pay players as little as possible, especially home-grown ones. It's true that footballers go where the money is 90% of the time, but a player should be advised where to go.

I'm in my best rigout for the PFA annual dinner, popping into the Punch & Judy pub in Covent Garden beforehand which is full of professional footballers – hundreds of them – though not players from the biggest Premier League teams. The mood is good, a load of lads in the prime of their life in £1,000 suits and looking as good as they'll ever look because they train every day. But there's sadness too, from former players at the function itself. They have their hard-luck stories, they hope for an opportunity – a chance chat with a manager who says they're after a number two, but the odds are stacked against them. They think they're rubbing shoulders with Robin van Persie because they're in the same union, but their lives are a million miles away from the elite players like him.

I can't afford to be proud. During the awards I make a

point of speaking to a few managers, once the waffling has finished from the top table. One manager is too preoccupied with a blonde half his age to give me too much time. He's brought her as his guest and I know she's not his wife. Five hundred people see this so he's either not bothered or hoping not to be rumbled. Or he'll just say that she's the club secretary, which she might be, one who has a very close working relationship with him.

The PFA dinner is not the place to pull – there is always the possibility that a newspaper may have arranged a honey trap. A couple of years ago, the *Daily Sport* sent a load of girls to the after party and they caused havoc. The footballers, as usual thinking through their dicks, never suspected that they were anything other than very good-looking girls who were gagging for it.

The girls all shagged players, but the one flaw in the operation was that the biggest names don't attend. Instead they bestowed their favours on mostly young pros who weren't really famous enough to make the front page. Any of the lucky players who had any sort of public profile received a phone call the next night from a *Sport* journalist.

'We believe you were with a girl last night.'

'No, I wasn't.'

'Are you sure? We've got quotes, we've got photos and CCTV.'

'I spoke to her, but nothing happened.'

'It's just that the girl is saying that you took her back to your room, where you had sex in four different positions and tried to stick a bottle up her backside. In fact, she's got a recording of it all on her phone.'

The story was printed, but because the names weren't big enough and the paper's credibility was so low, no one took much notice.

Another manager asks me what had gone wrong this season. I don't know if he means me personally or the team. I hope he doesn't mean me, but when I start answering about the team, the manager cuts in: 'And you?'

I tell him that I'd had a couple of niggles, but that I'd been fine for months now and was back at full fitness for the first time all season. He likes what he hears, I think. That's one to chase up in the summer if I'm not sorted.

On the pitch I have to focus solely on the present. We win an away game 2–1 at a club a place above us and that gives us a huge lift, both in terms of points and mentally. The winner is a penalty, taken towards the end of the game. Full credit to the lad who scored it. People have started murmuring about the cost of relegation to the Championship and stupid figures are mentioned, £50 to £60 million.

It shouldn't have been, but I let that thought get into my head as my teammate stepped up in front of the home end. Bang – he nailed it into the bottom left. Totally cool from twelve yards out. The gaffer is buzzing him, we all are.

Anyone can practise penalties and score nine out of ten times, but doing them under intense pressure is completely different. I've taken four in my professional career, scored two, missed one and had one saved. That millisecond when you realise that you've not scored, when the crowd hush ever so briefly, the point at which you say 'Fuck!' to yourself, is one of the worst feelings in football. I know of a lad who missed a penalty in a play-off final at Wembley. He'd been injured all season, but was brought on in the last minute of extra time. He was good at penalties and that's why his boss brought him on.

His wife was filming it on her phone. The clip is excruciating. You hear her saying: 'Please, please,' and then you hear: 'Oh, no!'

He hit the penalty sweetly and thought he'd scored. He couldn't understand why the ball pinged back past him. It had hit the post. His team lost on penalties, their opponents went up.

After one play-off semi-final, the boss of the team asked the fans to stay behind while his team practised penalties in front of thousands of fans. He didn't know that the chief scout of their play-off rivals was sitting in the main stand making notes on who put the ball where, which came in useful when the sides needed a penalty shoot-out in the next game. They won.

So we're 13th. We'd all settled for that as there's a four-point gap to 12th. And we'll get about £90,000 more each if we finish 13th rather than 17th.

On the subject of money, April is the month when the players' fines are collected. Not the ones for serious issues for breaches of discipline, the 'proper' fines. If you turn up for training smelling of alcohol then it's a week's wages. Same again if you are spotted out in a club or bar on a Thursday night, within forty-eight hours of a match.

These are the fines we agree among ourselves for lesser misdemeanours, brokered by the manager and the captain, though it's usually the manager and the assistant manager who will issue them.

The vice-captain will be the enforcer who will collect the money and put it into the players' pool, though I'm not sure where he stores thousands of pounds in notes all season. Near the end of the season, the money is counted, half of it goes to a local charity, the rest is for the players – maybe a big night out paid for by their fines.

Here's a selection of these fines at our club:

- dirty boots £50;
- parking in wrong space at the training ground £50;
- being late for team meeting. £200;
- wearing the wrong clothes £100;
- use of mobile phone in canteen or treatment room £50 (second offence £100);
- leaving newspaper in treatment room £50;
- not showering between training and eating £50;
- not having an ice bath after training £50;
- wearing a hat when eating £50

When Sven-Göran Eriksson took over at Manchester City in 2007, he asked to see the rules for the fines in front of all of his players. They were produced and were similar to the ones above. He had a quick read and ripped them up, explaining: 'There's only one rule here, respect.'

The Swede went on: 'You show it me and I'll show it you. If you don't I'll come down hard. If you crash on the motorway and you are late, that's fine. But if you are late three times and keep using the same excuses, there will be problems.'

That's a far more adult way of dealing with things than one manager, who issued the fines and also collected them.

He insisted that the money was going to charity, though nobody believed it, especially when a player saw a wedge of bank notes in his office.

Good-natured banter goes hand in hand with most of the fines, as well as pleas of innocence and victimisation. Some players really get the hump and there's a feeling that our former captain and fine enforcer took it all far too seriously. Which he did. He was a nice lad, but a bit square. He couldn't get in on the usual girls banter with the lads because he was such a goody-two-shoes. He'd wait by the door some days with his watch, fining everyone who was a bit late. At first it was funny, but then it was like having a copper in the dressing room. For a joke one day, I nicked his training top and stuck it in a bush near the door to the dressing room. Then a few of us kicked up a fuss and insisted that he was fined. He knew he was being set up, but couldn't do anything about it.

And he came a bit unstuck when the best player told him to stick his fine up his arse after he was nine minutes late for training. The captain tried to make fun of it, but the best player didn't see the joke. The captain toned his iron regime down a bit after that. He needed the best player onside.

Players are always falling out with each other. It can be momentarily during a match, or it can last a game and be settled by a handshake, with an acceptance that words are said in the heat of the moment. Sometimes it's more serious.

At one club, two strong-minded characters fell out. One, a midfielder, went mad at a striker for missing a chance. Strikers hate it when other players get on their back for missing chances – scoring is the hardest thing to do in football. Usually. The striker reacted and the argument was clear for all to see. They didn't shake hands at the end and just started blanking each other. Again, that doesn't need to be a huge problem. Fans sometimes think that all footballers are mates and it's simply not true. Nobody pretends that you're best mates; they are your teammates, but you're rivals with them for a start. And you know that when one leaves you'll probably never speak to them again, even though you say you will, but it's better to get on with your workmates, though there are exceptions. Andy Cole and Teddy Sheringham didn't get on and they didn't need to, but on the pitch they performed and there were no issues.

At my club, the two who fell out were neighbours who'd shared lifts to training together. Their partners got on. And all of a sudden they weren't speaking to each other, which was awkward. The manager should have banged their heads together, but he didn't and cliques began to form. You were either mates with one or the other and it did nothing for team spirit.

I watch some big Champions League games in the middle of April involving the biggest clubs in the world. Most of my teammates watch them too. You might think that's a given, but many, many professional footballers don't watch football and certainly wouldn't pay to watch it. They have their fill of it every day, training and playing. It's an intense life as a player. Strangers associate them with football and that's all they talk to them about, so you can excuse them for wanting a break from it. I know a couple of players who hate football – they're just very good at it. It's not the actual game they despise, but everything around it, the darker side of the game, the dodgy characters and back-stabbing.

Most pros would watch those Champions League quarter- and semi-finals though. I'm envious of the lads playing in those games, though not jealous. They've done really well to reach that level and most of them are there on merit. I'm happy to sit back and admire them. Playing there is a dream, they get to hear the Champions League music while standing on the pitch. That won't happen to me, but there was a chance earlier in my career when I was being talked about as a player who could play at that level. Talk is cheap and I never did, though I look at some players and think: 'He's no better than me, he was just fortunate and in the right place at the right time.' Texts will often fly around among team- mates, such as: 'How is he playing in the Champions League?' or one, which I particularly remember: 'He used to be my boot boy, now he's trying to mark Messi/Xavi/Ronaldo. Where did it all go wrong?'

To which I replied:

'You play Champions League every night, mate. On your PlayStation.'

We're about to enter May, the final month of the season where, for about six weeks, I'll be able to say 'yes' when people invite me to parties or events. When you play, you have to say 'no' almost all the time. No to weddings, birthdays and even funerals. Your closest friends and family will hold their weddings in June so that you can go – that's what my sister did, which I appreciated. They also understand that you will be unlikely to be able to commit to any big social event, so phrases like this are common: 'I realise you probably won't be able to do this, but . . .'

I missed the birth of my son, my first child, due to football.

I was away with England when I got a call late at night saying that my wife was about to go into labour. I told the manager and he was fine about me going to the hospital first thing in the morning, but said that I would not be able to play in the game if I disappeared the day before the match. I was woken with a text at 6 a.m. to congratulate me on becoming a father. So I missed out on one and didn't really think too much about it for a few years. I didn't make that mistake again with the second child.

You miss out on things, but you can't complain about the life that football gives you. You see the world – though you don't really see it. You go to wonderful cities where you are met at the airport and taken in an air-conditioned bus to a luxury hotel. I've been to places like Rome and Moscow and seen almost none of the sights, bar a training pitch, stadium and the view from the hotel (often out of the centre where it is quieter) and the road to the airport. I'd love to go back to these cities as a tourist and see them properly. I'm not sure other players think the same. Half haven't got a clue where they are. We stayed in Nice, France, once. A player asked me if it was called Nice because 'it's nice'. He pronounced both words exactly the same – and not how the French city should be pronounced. He was heard ringing his mates saying that he was 'in a place called Nice and it really is'.

Others would have no idea if Iceland was next to Cyprus or not, or whether Denver was near Derby.

We played one pre-season in America and a teammate asked what the weather was going to be like. I told him it would be freezing, despite knowing it was the middle of summer and over thirty degrees every day. He packed his big coat and jumpers. Everyone else took shorts and T-shirts. The same player told his girlfriend that he was getting on the plane and that he'd call her in 'three hours' when they landed. The flight was nine hours.

As well as watching Champions League games on television, I look around at the team going for promotion from the Championship with a slight feeling of envy. Being part of a team going up was one of the best feelings in my career.

Playing in a winning team is the ultimate high. Nothing to do with money or the increased win bonuses, but the sheer unadulterated buzz of winning week after week. Of going to away games and beating really good sides. Of seeing their fans so sick that they abuse you when you leave the field, but of also spotting an old timer clap you off the pitch because he knows that his team have been beaten by a quality side.

I've had a few really good runs in the Premier League. Been in the top four and enjoyed the buzz, but never been in a team which was expected to win everywhere, unlike my Championship outfit. That team was going for promotion, a nervy, exciting time where so much is on the line. You know that if you reach the Premier League then it's going to be a life-changing experience, but before that happens you get the thrill of going up, when the crowd are urging you on, when the city is jumping and everyone can't wait for the next match. The fans sing your name – a massive buzz for any player and there's not a wage slip in the world which can compete with it.

It feels like everything is coming together, that all the hard work is worthwhile. You go to games with a spring in your step, with a confidence that only comes from winning. You have a permanent Ready Brek glow. It's not arrogance, but confidence, a feeling that you will win no matter what. And it's wonderful.

There's another plus to getting direct promotion: you know when the season ends. Play-offs can add two weeks to the season when you're at your most knackered. We did get direct promotion, but there was a sting in the tail – my call up for an international game which had been arranged for the end of May. I didn't know whether to laugh or cry. I thought about pulling out of the squad even though I knew I was fortunate to be there.

I'd booked a family holiday, which cost £1,500 to change and I had to keep fit for another two weeks before playing the game, which was dire.

That's not going to happen this year and with us safe in mid-table, everything seems to be safely predictable – apart from where I'll be changing next season.

May

May is when football's trophies will be dished out for the chosen few. There will, inevitably, be none at our club. We might be in with a shout for a fair play award and the club might win a certificate for having the cleanest toilets or best pies, but that's it.

But we have our own internal award ceremony where local businesses, sponsors and box holders pay £1,500 per table of ten to be in the same room as us. Everyone has to dress formally, in black tie. A different player has been assigned to each table, with the captain seated with the main club sponsors and the youngest pro with a company which pays for a couple of advertising hoardings. I quickly scan who is on our table and sit down next to the person who looks the most normal. Turns out he's a politician of some kind. I'm a professional footballer – don't expect me to recognise anyone except David Cameron or Tony Blair. He asks me about politics and I'm struck by the realisation that nobody has asked me my opinion about politics ever before in my life. I think I've voted once. Politics is one topic of conversation which never comes up in a football dressing room. I think I'm typical. If 15% of footballers had voted I'd be surprised. Cuts in the NHS mean nothing to a £50k-a-week footballer, sadly.

I was once on a sponsors' table with someone I'd picked out in the crowd giving me stick months earlier. I'm good with faces, if not names. Fans think they're anonymous, they're not. You can't pick out someone on the third tier at Old Trafford, but it's much easier closer to the pitch. I felt tempted to ask if he gave me the wanker sign every week, but said nothing, not even when he was pissed and asking me to ring his mates.

It's a buzz if you get the club player of the year award and quite a pleasant night all told. The politician is excellent company, used to greasing the wheels of conversation. I win nothing, not that I deserve to.

The weather has improved slightly, provoking the most insecure player to spend £50,000 on a convertible Porsche which he drives to training with the roof down. He changes his car two or three times a season. He'll see the error of his ways, but probably not until he's skint in five years' time.

There's a story in a tabloid about one of our players. He's been shagging a stripper and she's done a kiss-and-tell. She's also been sleeping with another footballer and she's compared the two, with marks out of ten for technique, romance, size and intelligence. The other player gets 8s and 9s, ours gets 2s and 3s. He's slaughtered from the second the paper arrives in the dressing room. He can do nothing but take it on the chin and curse.

Players' relationships with women can be weird and far from the obvious. One of our players has got a super fan. Others might call her a stalker, but she's not. She's a normal-looking lady in her early thirties who watches him wherever he plays. She's followed him around three clubs now. I do wonder what would happen if he moved abroad. The player isn't having a relationship with her, but provides her with tickets and so she has his number. She always hangs around the team coach and has started dolling herself up a bit. He'll stop and say a quick hello and she might even introduce him to one of her mates. Never stop for more than a hello or you'll be there all day.

I think he's stuck between trying to help out a genuine fan whose attentions and interest are flattering and challenging himself not to misbehave. We've started to wind him up about her, like today on the way from the last away game from the season. She was there again, wishing him a good summer. He needs to talk about what's going on.

'Part of me really wants to shag her,' he said afterwards, 'but that will send her into full stalking mode. She actually doesn't pester me, she's very nice, but I know I could if I wanted to.'

He's actually in genuine turmoil about his number one fan. This is not an uncommon phenomenon, but confusing to the average professional used to girls who usually have one thing on their mind. If you think about it, there are plenty of male fans who follow a particular player, but her gender alters the dynamic. Well-dressed, nicely spoken, 'nice' women follow individual players and have a respectful, slightly romantic interest.

Other players are less discerning and, as the charming phrase goes, would mount anything female with a pulse.

I've never been stalked myself, but I was once on international duty and went to an English shopping centre with two teammates who were very famous. We went to get out of the hotel for a few hours and relieve the boredom. Within minutes they'd been recognised and thirty people began following them. I was slightly in awe, but I'm sure that it's a massive pain in the arse to have people following you when you just want to buy a paper.

We need to get our public appearances up in May. There's a girl at the club, a community liaison officer, who reports to the manager. She'll tell him if anyone has been skiving. And she'll tell all of us that we need to do two or three public appearances in the two weeks before the end of the season. Hospital visits, school presentation evenings, the usual. I agree to do a few more from people who've approached me independently, but I usually clear them with the club.

A friend of a friend has been sectioned in hospital. He's had a hard time and things have not gone well for him in recent years, though his own drug consumption hasn't helped. I'm not sure I can help either, but I agree when I'm asked if it would be possible to go and see him in hospital. Sort of like speaking to someone in a coma to see if a familiar voice will rouse them? Maybe not.

But I go along anyway. The lad is drugged up on medication but pleasant enough and capable of holding a conversation.

He'd been sectioned after being convinced that Sir Alex Ferguson was talking about him on the television, among other things. You shouldn't laugh, but I nearly did.

And I shouldn't have laughed when I was recognised by another patient, who looked like the seventies footballer Frank Worthington. It wasn't him. He came over and told me that he was good friends with several top-level former players, which I doubted. He also told me that he used to play for Nottingham Forest, which I also doubted. And he told me that while he was at Forest, training used to consist of him running six laps around the pitch before taking a penalty against Peter Shilton. If the player missed, then he had to do another six laps. I doubted that too.

His mobile went and he answered it as 'Frank'. He really did believe he was Frank Worthington. Another man told me that he was an Eskimo and asked me to throw snowballs at him. There wasn't much snow to hand on the unit.

There's never a dull moment when you play football, especially in May, football's silly season for rumours. They proliferate because a) there's uncertainty with contracts ending and b) nothing really happens. I was once linked with a move to Liverpool. Journalists were telling me that they were about to make a move. This was when Liverpool played in the Champions League. I asked my agent to find out if there was any truth in it and he told me that he'd call Liverpool. He told me that they were close to agreeing a fee with my club. And that's the last I heard. When they signed a player in my position a few months later, I gave up on Anfield.

MAY

A lot of agents tout for business in May. I got a call yesterday telling me that a few clubs were interested in me. I've given my verbal promise to the manager of the Premier League club I expect to be joining very soon and I didn't know the agent and was immediately mistrustful, though it would have been rude to ask him how he'd got my number. I don't normally answer numbers which I don't recognise, but I did with this one.

'X at West Brom is interested in you,' he said.

'That's interesting,' I replied. 'I know him well. I'll call him later.'

'Er, I've not spoken to him, but it has come from a good source,' he replied, his bluff having being called.

In the final week of our season, a man from the PFA comes to give a talk to us about life after football. This is a serious subject and all the players attend, though the lads who are in their early twenties pay almost no attention. No matter what you tell them, they think it's going to last for ever. The older lads are at the front, being advised on how to invest money. Pensions, portfolios and properties are mentioned. I look at these lads, the two who are out of contract and don't have the comfort of another year's contract or being five years younger like me. They need the advice. They both want to do 'their badges' and go into coaching in some form, which will mean weeks away at Lilleshall in the summer. There's an old boys' network in football where people help each other out – and not out of sympathy. If you've played with someone then you've worked with them every day. You've seen almost every trait of their personality and you know how they'll react in different conditions. That's why players employ former team-mates if they go into management.

We play our 38th and final league game of the season, at home. We're 14th and the team we're playing are 9th. No matter the result, we'll both stay in the same position. You might think that there's nothing to play for, but you'd play the game like any other. I'm not alone in wanting to finish the season on a high in front of our fans. That will be the last game they remember until next July – and possibly the last time they'll see me in the team's shirt. Not that they know it. I'm in a good mood as I warm up, though a comment of 'Oi, X, don't bother coming back next season' winds me up as I walk back to the dressing room. I'm tempted to go for the lad or at least say something, but I hold back. Now is not the time to have an assault on a fan to add to my CV.

We play well, draw 1–1 and finish 14th, which most of us would have settled for at the start of the season, though we would never had said that as it sounds under-ambitious.

We do a lap at the end of the game to thank the fans. Most of them stay behind to applaud us. We're encouraged to take our kids on the pitch and mine haven't shut up about it all week. I get them club shirts with their names on the back and my wife brings them down to the side of the tunnel at the end of the game. That's when the youngest one gets frightened and becomes too scared to go on the pitch in front of twenty-odd thousand people. I pick her up and carry her. The manager is feeling relieved too, the threat of relegation which made us nervous a month ago now seen off.

'Get the girls on too!' he says, gesturing towards the wives and girlfriends.

'Fuck that!' replies the captain, pointing to the area behind the goal. 'I'm not having those virgins telling my Mrs to get her tits out.'

So this may be the last time I walk on the pitch as a home-team player. I flash back to my times at this club with mixed memories.

Scarves are thrown at us, the fans sing 'We'll support you ever more' and my daughter tells me that she needs a wee. I tell her to hold on for ten minutes. The three-year-old son of another player doesn't tell his dad anything. He just has a shit, which isn't ideal as he's just out of nappies. One wife does make it onto the pitch then, the lad's mum, hurriedly drafted on to sort the mess out.

The away fans stay behind too and their players do half a lap of honour. You usually get big away followings on the final day of the season as it's their last trip before the summer. At some clubs the fans wear fancy dress on the last day of the season. I once found myself in the bizarre situation of getting abuse off Saddam Hussein, Buzz Lightyear (who cupped his ears to imply that I had big ears – I don't) and John Wayne calling me a 'cock' when I went to take a throw in before the away end. They were fans of a team who weren't so keen on me. I thought about flicking the vees back to them, but imagine the headlines? There was a gorilla standing with them, but King Kong, with nothing to prove, just looked at me.

And I've done a lap of honour after playing poorly in the final game of the poor season. Maybe five hundred fans – one in fifty – stayed behind. It felt more like a walk of shame.

The manager speaks to us one last time in the dressing

room. He seems happy enough and is probably confident of keeping his job. My opinion of him has dropped, partly because I'm not in his plans for the future, but also because he refused to sell me a year ago to a club who were offering me more to play in a better team. I knew they'd come in for me with a good offer and a transfer fee of several million pounds. The club didn't entertain it. Lucky them for not needing to. I would have gone, but the manager told me I'd be better where I am.

'What do you want to go there for?' asked the manager in a conversation at the training ground with him and the sporting director, himself an ex-manager.

'We'll be better than them next season. No question about that.'

'What about a new contract then?' I asked.

'Don't be so paranoid and insecure,' replied the sporting director. 'You'll be better in a year because you'll be the hottest property at the club. Everyone will want you and you'll only have a year left. The world will be your oyster.'

Had I done as well this season as last that would have been the case. I would have been in a really strong position with a year left to run on my contract. But I didn't. And we weren't better than the team who came in for me. They finished in a European spot, we finished 14th. I can't help but wonder that I could be about to play European football, one year into a three- or four-year contract. But football is full of 'what ifs'.

I could say something to the manager, who still hasn't spoken to me face-to-face about my future. It's a conversation I'm never likely to have with him. I could kick up a fuss, but

I take the advice of a former pro who once told me: 'Don't ever burn your bridges in football. What goes around comes around.'

I took that on board and while it's impossible not to fall out with some people, I've always tried to make sure that as many people as possible thought highly of me at every club I've been associated with.

As well as the club Player of the Year awards, the players are asked to go to the supporters' end of season awards in a function room at the club a day or two after the final game. It's more informal and players can wear what they want. They'll ask the gaffer how long they have to stay for and the gaffer will say: 'I want you there for at least an hour,' or, 'Stay until half nine when the awards are done and dusted'. As with the club's Player of the Year, anyone getting the fans' Player of the Year award is chuffed. They're the people who've spent their hard-earned.

An afternoon getting leathered in the pub before spending the night signing autographs is not a good mix and I've seen it all go wrong a few times.

Once, four players drank themselves stupid and then went off to the fans' do. The manager could see they'd had a few and got his assistant to keep an eye on them. Not even he could stop the players loudly booing the gaffer when he got up to speak. The manager was furious and fined them all a week's wages. The club received a bag of letters which pointed out how this was all down to the ending of National Service, banning the cane and extravagant players' salaries.

I've heard worse, like stories of one or two who've done recreational drugs all summer, starting with several lines at the fans' party, knowing they won't be tested for a few months.

The end of season do is one place where the players try their best with the fans, though. They are usually held in a function room at the club and you try and show your appreciation for the people who have supported you and spent their money watching you.

These functions usually go well, but not if you've had a bad season. A mate of mine played for a club who had just been relegated from the Premier League. He said the atmosphere was tense all night, with fans having a dig at the manager who wasn't one to turn the other cheek. It finished with the manager and his hardman physio going toe-to-toe against six fans in the car park. He didn't last much longer in the job which shows that no matter what you think about fans, you should always avoid hitting them.

We've arranged to have a players' night out after the fans' function, with the festivities being paid for by the proceeds of our fines. We get cabs from the ground to a city centre bar/club which has reserved a section for us. There are bottles of champagne waiting in buckets, beers and spirits on the table for us when we arrive, very thirsty, at 10 p.m.

Two lads have brought their dads along. They've both travelled from the other end of the country to stay with their lad for a few days away from the wife. One of them is an HGV driver who speaks in an accent so strong that none of us can understand him. He tries to order a pint of bitter in the club, but we get him on the Jagerbombs. His son takes him home just after eleven, not long after he'd slumped in his seat pissed out of his head. The player did say that his dad liked a drink.

The other dad looks like a fish out of water in the nightclub – and not only because he's wearing three-quarter-length pants with an elasticated waist. Unaware that it's waiter service, he asks the lads what they want to drink and returns from the bar clutching three pints. Someone creeps up behind him and pulls his pants down. The dad stands there, holding three pints with his pipe swinging. I don't know who looked more surprised, the player or his dad. The player at least went to help his mortified dad, relieving him of his drinks so that he could at least restore some semblance of dignity by pulling his pants up.

There will be a few players on the night out who I'll never see again in my life. We've got no more club commitments where we all have to be together. There might be a charity golf day, but not always. I'm probably on my way and some of them definitely are as well. You promise each other that you'll keep in touch but you know in your heart of hearts you won't. I embrace a couple of lads in drink and suddenly the lows of this season don't seem low and it all seems alright, like we've been on a wonderful adventure. You forget the bad times.

A few days later, I watch the FA Cup final, but not with the enthusiasm I had as a kid. The team who knocked us out are in it. They all get their medals at the end and we've got none. They're in the minority in football, on a different level to us.

A day or two after the final game of the season, players report to the training ground to collect their belongings for the summer and be weighed by the fitness staff. A fitness coach will give you a twenty-five-page booklet which is your training regime for the summer – and 90% of players will throw it straight into the boot of their car and never look at it. It won't be my holiday reading.

Once you've been weighed, the tradition is to go straight to the pub – you're free for the summer and the inviting prospect of really letting yourself go beckons.

I'll always find my boot boy and give him a few quid, usually £100 as thanks for cleaning my boots all season. He's one of the apprentices and I've encouraged him in his own career all season, always asking him about games and results. I've always made sure that I've had time for him and I'm genuinely interested in his career. He earns £80 a week so the £100 makes a difference. I was a boot boy myself once and as much as you hate cleaning out the dressing rooms and being the subject of myriad tiresome, painful and humiliating 'initiation rituals', the chores and the bullying were character building.

I didn't always get it right, though. As well as cleaning the boots every day, I had to pack for away games. Boots, bibs, cones and balls were all loaded into a metal skip, which went on the coach.

I once forgot the balls for an away game in Sheffield.

The kitman came to check that I'd packed everything and I said that I had. He even read out what I had packed and I nodded to 'cones', 'balls', 'bibs'.

I'm told that, upon unloading everything, the kitman swore: 'he hasn't packed the balls. The little shit hasn't packed the fucking balls!'

He rushed out to buy new balls, but the best he could do

were some £14.99 lightweight adidas ones from Toys R Us. They're fine when you're twelve, not a professional footballer. There's a huge difference and you become accustomed to very expensive balls which are perfectly weighted.

The players noticed straight away and found the whole thing funny. The manager and the kitman didn't.

The first I knew about it was in training when the first team returned and the kitman came up to me and said: 'You're a fucking wanker and I'll say it to your face. And if you were a bit older you'd be getting more than words, you thick fucker!'

I'm kinder to my boot boy, though I might not be so happy if he'd forgot to pack my boots. I gave him my number at the start of the season and I tell him that I might not be around next season, that if he ever needs to call me, he has my number.

Sadly, not even the apprentices at the biggest club do the boots anymore, but those are cleaned by the small army working out of the kitman's room.

The kitman helps me with my stuff as I clear my locker. He's got a good idea that I'll be off, but nothing is said. Living in a state of flux is normal for a footballer.

And it's not like other players aren't clearing their lockers out; it's the norm for every player at every club. I don't find any pigs' heads in my locker. I see a few of the other players and wish them well. I know that some are leaving and we promise to keep in touch. We won't. There are others who I'll be quite happy if I never see in my life again.

The first few weeks after the season has ended are carefree bliss for a player. You can eat what you want and do what you want after nine months of almost every day of your life being regimented. Most players binge on the junk food which is usually barred. They'll worry about the consequences later.

One teammate loves nothing more than going out in his home town of Birmingham with his best mate from school who now works as a plumber. He takes the day off work and they have a full English breakfast in a Wetherspoon's pub full of all-day drinkers and spend a stress-free day talking and drinking Guinness. He doesn't have to worry about picking up any cones or any matches, only what sauce he'll have on his kebab before he goes home. He looks forward to that day all year like a kid looks forward to Christmas. But that's the only time he does it, like a tradition which he says he'll keep going for as long as they are both alive. Some players hit the bottle much, much harder and not the tomato sauce.

The foreign lads usually leave England at the first opportunity, not to be seen until the first day of pre-season. Other players will leave the city and go to their 'base', the city where they are from. It all depends on their circumstances, where their wife is from and whether they have kids in school or not.

For me, it's the most chilled-out part of the year. I really appreciate the break from football and feel like I need it both mentally and physically. My wife understands this and leaves me to it. She doesn't get on my case if I go to bed at two and wake up at ten. My kids love having me about more at weekends. I sleep a lot better too, free, temporarily, from worry. I'm not even worried about getting a new club just yet because I know something will get sorted.

I might watch a bit of the World Cup or European

championships on TV with mates in the pub, but football is low down on my list of priorities.

The lads' trip to Vegas is scheduled to go ahead, while I'm going back to Portugal with the family. One former colleague was a little too desperate to get to Vegas. Several teammates were going, but his girlfriend had booked a holiday for the two of them the following week so he couldn't go on the lads' holiday. The close season is the one time of the year when you can give your wife or girlfriend proper attention. Or spoil them a bit to shut them up, in dressing-room parlance.

The boys arrived in Vegas and texted him non-stop about how good it was and how he was missing out. He decided to join them and sneaked out of the house in the night. He left his girlfriend a note saying that he had to go away and didn't want to disturb her, then stupidly updated his Facebook status to 'Viva Las Vegas'. He then drove to the airport and paid a fortune for a flight. What's a few grand to someone who earns five figures a week?

Twelve hours later he was by the pool, high-fiving his teammates when he got a call from a close friend back home who told him he'd better come home. His girlfriend had smashed the house up. He came back to a wreck. They split soon after.

There are still six players in our dressing room going to Vegas next week, but the trip has continued to cause all kinds of problems among wives and girlfriends. They've all found out about it by now. Two are threatening to leave their partners. I doubt they will.

There are hazards for the players who manage to stay a little longer on holiday. One player, a Premier League captain, was drunk on a stag do in Portugal when he stood on some glass as he tried to throw the stag into the sea. He missed the first six weeks of the season. He told his manager that he'd tripped on some stairs.

I've had a few mishaps on holiday myself. I knackered my back on a water slide in Spain two weeks before I was due to return for training. If you're injured then you have to go to the training ground every day and nobody wants to do that in the summer except a couple of busybodies who are the manager's pets and despised by the other players.

I told people at the club that I'd hurt my back doing weights at home and had to spend the first week training apart from the main group as I recuperated. I wasn't the only one away from the main group – anyone who comes back seriously overweight has to train alone. It's the ultimate humiliation on several levels and I've only seen it happen three times. You train alone because a player a stone overweight would be more likely to pick up an injury if he tried to train at full pelt. He'll be sent on fat-burning runs and told that he can't be considered in the manager's plans until he's fit. He went a little easier the following summer, but only a little.

I walk to the car park after saying goodbye to the staff I like. Not a 'proper' goodbye with hugs and that, but even so it makes me feel a little emotional. I can't be bothered speaking to others, the ones who were all over me when I was playing well but decidedly cold when I wasn't.

Unless you're a superstar, one of the very, very few in football who reach the top and stay there, one of the very few who gets a testimonial, there is no send-off when you leave a club. The reality is that you move around several times, part of a huge turnover in an industry where three years at the same club is considered a stretch. Professional football is an individual game played in a team context and every player cares most about his own career.

I turn the key in the ignition and drive off, without looking back.